WAY TO PLAY

SOCCER

Prima Publishing, Rocklin, CA 95677

Printed and bound in Spain

98 10 9 8 7 6 5 4 3 2

Library of Congress Cataloging-in-Publication Data

Stewart, Peter, 1942-
        Way to play soccer: the full-color guide to maximizing your skills / Peter
Stewart
        p. cm.
        Includes index.
        ISBN 0-7615-0028-6 (pbk.)
        1. Soccer. I. Title.
GV943.S754 1995   95-3351
796.332--dc20   CIP

Illustrations by Oliver Frey

PHOTOGRAPHIC ACKNOWLEDGMENTS
The publishers would like to thank the following sources for their kind permission
to reproduce the pictures used in this publication:
Allsport; Colorsport and Bob Thomas Sports Photography.

THE AUTHOR
PETER STEWART was the editor of *Shoot*—Britain's best-selling soccer magazine – for
eight years. He then became managing editor of the football group at IPC Magazines
Ltd., which included *Shoot, World Soccer, Soccerstars* and *90 Minutes,* all top-selling
soccer titles. He is now freelance editorial consultant to the football group and also
edits the West Ham United F.C. Matchday program and has compiled several reference
books. He is an enthusiastic supporter of the world-famous Coerver Coaching program
and has promoted the development of this coaching system in the U.K. He is also the
U.K. representative for the Dallas International Youth Tournament and a founder
member of the Association of Soccer Coaches and Teachers, and works closely
with leading soccer personalities.

WAY TO PLAY

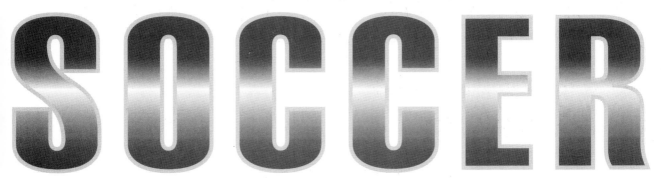

SOCCER

THE FULL-COLOR GUIDE
TO MAXIMIZING YOUR SKILLS

Peter Stewart

Prima Publishing
P.O. Box 1260
Rocklin, CA 95677
(916) 632-4400

PRIMA

Contents

Introduction

SOCCER is one of the easiest games to play. It is also the most popular and exciting contact sport in the world with over 117 million players—among them six million women—spread throughout 175 countries. It is watched by billions of fans in stadia and on television throughout the world. The 1994 World Cup, the first finals to be staged in the USA, attracted a world-wide TV audience of 31.5 billion.

"The Beautiful Game," as soccer was once described by Pele, perhaps the greatest player of all-time, is also "The People's Game." It can be played anywhere and on almost any kind of surface. The great Pele is just one of hundreds of top stars who learned their skills kicking a tennis ball, or tin can, along a beach or back-street in some remote town or village around the world. The game gives players the opportunity to combine individual skills with the strength and discipline of teamwork... and spectators the thrill and passion of watching players and teams display the different tactics and variety of techniques that make it so special.

This book, Way-To-Play Soccer, is aimed at providing players of all ages and skill with a better understanding of the game. Even today's great players (such as Ryan Giggs, Alan Shearer, Roberto Baggio, Dennis Bergkamp, Jürgen Klinsmann and Romario) need to practice and work hard at perfecting their skills. They also need good knowledge of the Laws of the Game to play the game in the right spirit, promote fair play and prove a worthy inspiration to young players hoping to follow in their footsteps.

The first section of this book explains in detail the 17 Laws of the Game, including the least understood and most controversial of them all, the offside rule. The second section provides hundreds of tips that are of enormous benefit to all young players. All the game's skills, tactics and techniques are brought to life with specially commissioned full-color illustrations and diagrams, and there are tips on passing, shooting, heading, trapping, dribbling, tackling, plus a special chapter devoted to goalkeeping. The book also includes an analysis of advanced techniques for experienced players, such as the glancing header, the overhead kick and the swerved pass with the outside of the foot.

The third section comprises of a study of soccer tactics, including modern-game team formations, attacking and defensive strategies, and set-piece plays, such as corner-kicks, free-kicks and throw-ins. The book is packed with Way-To-Play tips and photographs of today's top players in action. Finally, there's a two-page glossary of key soccer terms and an index.

Reading this book and using it to practice the skills and techniques explained in its pages will help you get more satisfaction out of the game and become a better player—whatever skill level you are aiming to achieve.

PETER STEWART

The Rules of the Game

TO play and enjoy soccer you should be fit, have good balance, be prepared to practice to improve your skills, and understand the Laws of the Game. Without a sound knowledge of the 17 Laws of the Game players and spectators will never really appreciate and be able to develop the finer points of the game.

1 THE FIELD OF PLAY

Dimensions

The soccer field must be rectangular to insure the flow of play between the two goals. Its length must not be more than 130 yards nor less than 100 yards. The width must not be more than 100 yards or less than 50 yards. However, the field cannot be square.

The Goal Area

This is generally known as the "six-yard box" and is formed by measuring six yards from the inside of each goalpost along the goal line. Two lines then extend six yards into the Field Of Play at right angles to the goal line. These lines are connected by a line parallel to the goal line. The main purpose of the Goal Area is to indicate where goal kicks should be taken.

The Goals

These are the most important pieces of equipment on the Field of Play. They are placed on the center of each goal line and consist of two upright posts, eight yards apart, joined by a horizontal crossbar which must be eight feet from the ground. The width and depth of the goalposts and crossbar must not exceed five inches. They must be made of wood, metal or other approved material and are white so they can easily be seen. Nets are attached to the posts and crossbars. They should be properly pegged down at the sides and behind the goal to ensure they don't sag because this could impede the goalkeeper, and allow the ball to pass underneath.

The Penalty Area

At each end of the field, two lines are drawn at right-angles to the goal line, 18 yards from each goalpost. These extend 18 yards into the Field of Play and are joined by a line drawn parallel to the goal line. This defines the area in which the goalkeeper can handle the ball. A mark is then made within each penalty area 12 yards from the mid-point of each goal line. This is called the penalty spot. From this spot an arc of a circle with a radius of ten yards is drawn outside the penalty area. This arc indicates the mimimum distance that players must be from the ball when a penalty kick is being taken.

Way-To-Play Tips

Check lines

As soon as you arrive at the field to play your match, check to insure that all lines are clearly marked. Occasionally, lines will not be clear due to bad weather, or because no one has bothered to re-line after the last game. Also check that the lines are not rutted. Ruts can cause injury if players twist their ankles in them.

Marking

The Field of Play is marked with clear and distinctive (usually white) lines, not more than five inches (12cm) wide. The longer boundary lines are called sidelines and the shorter lines are the goal lines. Corner flags at least five feet high with non-pointed tops, to reduce the risk of injury to players, are placed at each corner of the field. Similar flags may be placed at the midfield line, not less than one yard outside the sideline. These are optional. The Field of Play is divided into two equal halves by a midfield line. The center of the field is indicated with a suitable mark for the kick-off. From this a circle with a ten-yard radius is marked around it. This is known as the center circle, and enables the referee to insure the opposing team is standing at least ten yards from the ball at the kick-off.

The Corner Area

A small quarter-circle with a one-yard radius is drawn from each corner flagpost inside the Field Of Play. This shows the area where the ball must be placed when a corner kick is taken.

② THE BALL

The ball must be spherical and made of leather, or other approved materials. The circumference must be between 27–28 inches and weigh 14–16 oz. It should be carefully inspected by the referee before a match to insure it is not too hard, or too soft. The ball should not be changed during a game unless authorized by the referee. Spare balls should always be available.

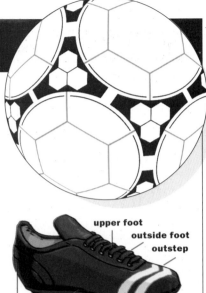

③ NUMBER OF PLAYERS

A match is played by two teams, each consisting of 11 players, one of whom must be the goalkeeper. In addition substitutes, usually three, can be used depending on the rules of the game being played. Substitutes can only enter the Field Of Play during a stoppage in the game, and after a signal from the referee. The substitute must enter the Field Of Play at the halfway line after the player being replaced has left. Once substituted, a player cannot return to the game. If a player is ordered off after play has started he cannot be replaced. In most major club competitions around the world a goalkeeper is named among the substitutes. But any of the other players can change places with the goalkeeper, provided that the referee's permission is obtained and the player wears the appropriate jersey.

upper foot

outside foot

outstep

heel

inside foot

instep

toe

Shoes may have studs or bars for grip that conform to rigid standards to protect other players. This is a left shoe pictured above and below.

④ PLAYERS' EQUIPMENT

The basic requirement of a player is a shirt (or jersey), shorts, socks, shinguards and soccer shoes. There are two main types of shoe: the molded sole for hard, dry fields and the screw-in stud shoe for softer surfaces. The advantage of screw-in studs is that they can be changed to suit the conditions. Longer studs are used for wet and muddy surfaces and shorter ones for dry grounds. They are made of plastic, rubber, aluminum or other suitable material. Studs prevent players from slipping.

The players of one team wear the same colored shirts, which must be different from the opposition. The goalkeeper must wear a distinctive colored jersey to distinguish him from the other players and referee. He may also wear gloves to improve his grip on the ball, and occasionally a cap to keep the sun out of his eyes. Numbers are generally worn on the backs of shirts. Players must not wear anything that is likely to be a danger to other players.

Players should always take a pride in their appearance.

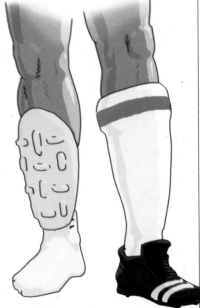

Shin guards must be worn to protect a player's shin.

5 REFEREES

Way-To-Play Tips

Ball work
Always carry a spare ball, pump and valve adaptors, you'd be surprised how many teams don't. The referee must check that the match and spare balls are correctly inflated. If a ball is too hard it will bounce excessively, too soft and the ball will be "lifeless" with little bounce, making it difficult to pass accurately.

Check your cleats
Although the wearing of shin guards is now compulsory, players are still hurt by sharp cleats. Be sure your cleats do not have any sharp edges, or else a harmless tackle could result in a bad injury.

A referee is appointed to control the game. His authority and the powers granted to him under the Laws of the Game take effect as soon as he enters the Field Of Play. The referee enforces the Laws of the Game; keeps a record of the game; acts as time-keeper and can add on time lost through injuries or other causes; stops the game at injuries and fouls; can caution or eject offending players; may suspend or end the game before normal time because of bad weather, trouble caused by spectators, or any other incident he considers such action necessary. The referee's decision on the Field Of Play is final and should not be disputed. The referee will wear colors distinctive from the shirts worn by the two opposing teams. No person other than the players may enter the Field Of Play without the referee's permission. A referee will normally take the following items out with him on to the Field Of Play—pencil, spare pencil, notebook, whistle, spare whistle, coin, stopwatch, wristwatch, yellow and red cards.

Referees have to pass an exam which tests their knowledge of the Laws of the Game, and courses are held regularly. Players are encouraged to go on a referee's course so that they get a better understanding of soccer. It is amazing, but many top players do not know all the Laws of the Game.

George Courtney was England's top referee in the late 1980s/early 1990s and officiated in the 1990 World Cup.

6 LINESMEN

Two linesmen are appointed for each game to assist the referee to control the game in accordance with the Laws. The linesmen, one on each sideline, indicate to the referee when the ball is out of play and which team has a corner kick, goal kick or throw-in.

When a linesman sees an infringement of the Laws, he will raise his vividly colored flag to indicate the foul, and the referee will then choose whether or not to act on this signal.

One of the linesmen's most important tasks is to watch for offside because they are in the ideal position to judge.

Linesmen flag signals: throw-in (above) and substitution (right).

The linesman indicates (clockwise from the top) offside: when play has stopped; the position on the far side of the field; centre of the field; and near side of the field.

7 GAME DURATION

The duration of the game shall be two equal periods of 45 minutes, unless otherwise mutually agreed upon. At the referee's discretion, allowance can usually made for time lost through injury, time-wasting or substitutions. Time will also be allowed for the taking of a penalty kick at, or after, the end of normal time in either half. Halftime should not exceed 15 minutes. At the World Cup finals, and during some televised games, the half-time break is further extended.

8 THE START OF PLAY

To start a game, the two captains toss a coin for choice of ends, or for the right to kick off. Before whistling for the kick-off to be taken, the Referee should ensure the ball is stationary on the center spot. Opponents must not come into the center circle (within ten yards of the ball) until the ball is kicked. On the referee's whistle, the game is started by a player kicking the ball forward. Once played the ball must travel one circumference before being touched by another player. The player kicking off must not play the ball again until it has been touched by another player. The game should be restarted in the same manner, although at the start of the second half the teams should change ends. The team which didn't kick off in the first half has the second-half kick-off.

9 BALL IN AND OUT OF PLAY

The ball is out of play when (a) the whole of the ball has crossed the goal or sidelines, either on the ground or in the air and (b) when the game has been stopped by the referee. The ball is in play at all other times, including when it rebounds off the goalposts, crossbar, corner flags or the referee.

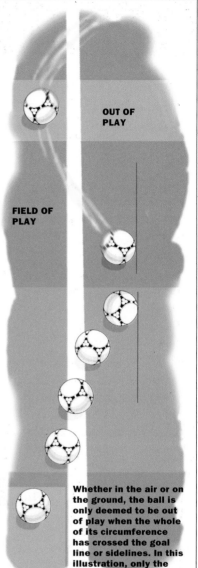

OUT OF PLAY

FIELD OF PLAY

Whether in the air or on the ground, the ball is only deemed to be out of play when the whole of its circumference has crossed the goal line or sidelines. In this illustration, only the balls on the red lines are out of play.

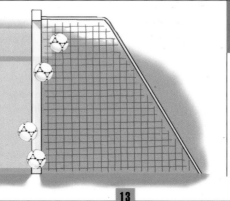

In this illustration, only the ball in the pale blue area at the top counts as having crossed the goal line. If the goalkeeper were to stop any of the others at their current positions, the goal will have been saved.

10 SCORING

A goal is scored when the whole ball has crossed the goal line, either on the ground or in the air, between the goalposts and under the crossbar. The team scoring the most goals wins the game. If the number of goals scored is equal the result is a draw.

THE Offside Law is the most misunderstood and controversial of all the rules. Many players, even top internationals, are often unaware exactly when they are offside. The first thing to remember is that your position when you receive the ball is irrelevant. What matters is your position when the ball is actually played forward.

If, at the moment the ball is passed, there are less than two defenders between an attacker and the goal, the attacker is offside—remember the goalkeeper usually counts as one of the two defenders. When you are attacking if you are level with the last defender with only the goalkeeper in front of you, you are not offside.

Exceptions

There are three occasions when your positioning is not relevant, when the ball is played. They are:

(1) from a goal kick; or
(2) from a throw-in; or
(3) from a corner kick.

However, in each case, as soon as the ball is touched by a teammate you can be offside.

You can be offside from a free kick, a drop-kick or a throw from your goalkeeper, too. You can also be offside if the ball bounces off a teammate and goes forward to you, even if an opposing defender is the last player to deliberately kick or head the ball. If a teammate's forward pass touches a defender and goes to you in an offside position with no defenders closer to the goal line, you are still offside.

There are times when an attacker is not offside with no defenders closer to the goal line. These are when the ball is passed backward by a teammate who is already closer to goal than you are (but remember when you then shoot for goal that this teammate may be in an offside position). You are not offside if you are in your own half of the field when the ball is played.

BELOW AND OPPOSITE: four examples of onside and offside positions. Yellow lines represent the path of the ball, red lines the movement of players. Attackers are in red, defenders in blue shirts and yellow shorts. The goalkeeper is in gray.

Player (A) is OFFSIDE because there is only one defender (the goalkeeper) between him and the goal when the ball is played.

A new rule brought in for the 1994 World Cup Finals states that a player shall not be declared offside unless (when in an offside position) he makes an active attempt to play the ball. Basically you can now stand anywhere as long as you are not in line with the goalkeeper. You should not be called offside unless the ball is passed to you by a teammate, or you make a deliberate run toward the ball.

Interfering with play

At this point it is worth thinking about phrase "not interfering with play." Normally the only time this is the case is when the ball is crossed backward from the wings. On a corner, for instance, the corner kicker may be the closer to the goal line than any defender but clearly not interfering with play.

Player (A) is OFFSIDE because although defender (X) is closer to the goal, goalkeeper (Y) defender (Z) are actually in front of (A), so there is only one defender between the attacker and the goal.

Player (A) is ONSIDE. Although only the goalkeeper is closer to the goal line than the front two attackers, because Player (B) has run past two defenders (from B1–B2), the eventual cross has been pulled back to Player (A).

If you know you are in an offside position as an attack develops, you may think you can step off the field and take yourself out of the game. You can try it... but the referee may want to card you for leaving the field without permission.

If you are injured, the referee or the linesman may consider that you are "not interfering with play," but if you then get up and run after the ball, the linesman is sure to raise the flag.

Free kick

If a player is declared offside, the referee will award an indirect free kick to the opposing team from the spot where the infringement occurred, unless the offense is committed by a player in the opponents' goal area. In this case, the free kick should be taken from any point within the goal area.

Offside Trap

This tactic is often deployed by defenders to put attackers offside deliberately. While marking the attackers as they wait for a pass, the defenders will suddenly move out in a line as the ball is about to be played, stranding them in an offside position, or forcing them to play the ball back toward their own goal.

Using this tactic successfully requires good teamwork and discipline. If played properly it can be an effective method of stopping attacks and frustrating forwards. But don't get complacent. The trap can be beaten by an attacker dribbling the ball through it, or quick passing.

Way-To-Play Tips

Be aware

If you are your team's most forward attacker it is your responsibility to insure you stay onside by (a) remaining behind the ball; (b) keeping at least two opponents between yourself and the goal line; and (c) keeping well clear of the action if you find yourself in an offside position.

Timing

Practice making timed runs to beat your opponents' offside trap. If you time your run perfectly and the pass is a good one you may have a breakaway.

Accept the decision

In the vast majority of cases the linesman is going to make the right decision. Whatever you say to him (which might be punished with a caution), however, he won't change his mind, so accept his decision—even if you are certain it is not the right one—and go on the with game.

An attacker scores while a teammate is standing in an offside position. But because he is not interfering with play, he should not be penalized for offside and the goal will stand.

12 FOULS AND MISCONDUCT

LAW 12 was not devised to discourage the physical effort needed to play the game. It provides a code of discipline to enable you to display your skills in a physical contact game by protecting you against unnecessary force and foul play. Law 12 comprises three parts: (a) Major Offenses, (b) Other Offenses and (c) Misconduct.

The Major Offenses

There are nine major offenses which, if committed intentionally, are penalized by awarding a direct free kick to the opposing team. Eight of the nine offenses are concerned with physical fouls against opponents. If a defending player intentionally commits any one of these nine offenses on an attacker within the penalty area, a penalty kick will be awarded.

The major offenses are:

(1) Kicking, or attempting to kick an opponent;

(2) Tripping an opponent using the legs; by stooping in front of, or behind an opponent;

(3) Jumping at an opponent;

(4) Charging in a violent or dangerous manner;

(5) Charging an opponent from behind in a violent or dangerous manner (unless the opponent is guilty of obstruction);

(6) Striking, attempting to strike, or spitting at an opponent;

(7) Holding an opponent with the hand or arm;

(8) Pushing an opponent

(9) Handling the ball with any part of the hand or arm.

Other Non-major Offenses

Offenses for which the correct award is an indirect free kick are:

(1) Dangerous play (for example attempting to kick the ball while it is being held by the goalkeeper, attempting to kick a ball close to the head of an opponent)

(2) Charging an opponent fairly, but while not attempting to play the

Sweden's Klaus Ingesson is brought down from behind.

ball (shoulder charging an opponent fairly, but when the ball is not within playing distance)

(3) Obstruction (blocking an opponent's path to the ball when it is not within playing distance)

(4) Charging the goalkeeper (unless he is holding the ball, obstructing an opponent, or has gone outside his goal area)

(5) Goalkeeper not releasing the ball into play properly (when the keeper takes more than four steps while holding, bouncing or throwing the ball in the air before releasing it. After releasing the ball, the goalkeeper is not allowed to touch it again with his hands until it has been played by

Whether intentional or not, tripping up an opponent is foul play. Here the culprit is clearly not aiming for the ball in the tackle.

another player. He is, however, permitted to play the ball with his feet)

(6) Time-wasting by the goalkeeper (if the referee considers the keeper is holding on to the ball for an unreasonable amount of time, or using other tactics considered by the referee to be wasting time and giving an unfair advantage to his own team)

(7) If a goalkeeper touches the ball with his hand, or hands, to control it after it has been deliberately kicked to him by a teammate. Again this was brought in to stop time-wasting.

(8) Offside (see Pages 14-15)

The "Professional Foul"

If you are denied an obvious goal scoring opportunity by an opponent deliberately handling the ball, or by unfairly impeding your path to goal, the referee must call this a serious foul and eject the offender from the Field Of Play.

Misconduct

All players should understand the Laws of the Game to avoid committing fouls; accept the referee's decisions without argument, and conduct themselves as sportsmen. Referees will show the yellow card, caution players and award the opposing team an indirect free kick if they:

(1) enter, or re-enter the Field Of Play after the game has started, or leave the Field Of Play during the game's progress (except through accident) without first gaining permission from the referee;

(2) show by word or action, dissent from any decision given by the referee;

(3) are guilty of ungentlemanly conduct;

(4) persistently infringe the Laws of the Game.

Players will be shown the red card and be ejected, if in the opinion of

A player will be shown the red card, and ejected, for serious foul play.

the referee they are guilty of:

(1) violent conduct, or serious foul play;

(2) using foul and abusive language;

(3) committing a second cautionable offense after having received a caution.

If play is stopped because a player is ordered from the Field Of Play for an offense without a separate breach of the Law having been committed, the game will be resumed by an indirect free kick awarded to the opposing team from the place where the infringement occurred.

Dangerous play, such as kicking at a high ball in another player's face, is an offense which will be penalized.

Way-To-Play Tips

Ungentlemanly conduct

Often a player will shout "My ball!" or "Leave it!" when going for the ball. Opponents can be distracted by this and hesitate when challenging for the ball. If you do yell always use a player's name, for example: "Bill King's ball!" or "Goalkeeper's ball!"
Holding an opponent back by his shirt, or climbing on his back to gain extra height are two other examples of unfair play. Above all, remember a referee's decision is final—don't agrue with him or his linesmen, or you could get carded for dissent.

13 FREE KICKS

A free kick is either direct or indirect from the spot where the foul occurred. A direct free kick is one from which the player taking the kick can score if the ball goes directly into the opponents' goal. An indirect free kick is one from which a goal cannot be scored until the ball has been touched by another player. To indicate that a free kick is indirect the referee will raise one arm above his head.

At any free kick opponents must be at least ten yards from the ball, except when a direct free kick has been awarded less than ten yards from the goal. Opponents may then stand between the goalposts.

The referee is clearly indicating why he wanted a free kick against an offending player.

If the defending team is awarded a free kick in its own penalty area, the ball must be kicked out of the area and no opponents may enter the area until the kick is taken.

The ball must be stationary at a free kick, and it must be touched by another player before the kicker is allowed to touch it a second time.

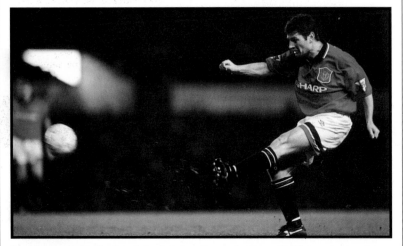

Manchester United's Dennis Irwin takes the perfect penalty kick.

14 THE PENALTY KICK

A penalty kick often proves crucial in a game. A penalty proved to be a World Cup Final winner for Germany in the 1990 final when Brehme converted his in the 85th minute to give his team a victory over Argentina.

Any offense committed by the defending team that results in a direct free kick inside their own penalty area is punished by a penalty kick.

A penalty kick is taken from the penalty spot. When it is taken all players, with the exception of the goalkeeper and the player taking the kick, must stand outside the penalty area at least ten yards from the penalty spot.

The goalkeeper must stand on the goal line without moving his feet until the ball is kicked. The player taking the kick must kick the ball forward. Once he's taken the kick he cannot play the ball a second time until it has been touched by another player.

A goal can be scored direct from a penalty kick. Time can be extended at half time or the end of the game to allow a penalty kick to be taken, or retaken. The kick is retaken if:

(1) the defending team breaks the Law and a goal is not scored
(2) the attacking team, with the exception of the kicker, infringes and a goal is scored
(3) there are infringements by players of both teams. If the kicker breaks the Law, for example playing the ball twice, the defending team is awarded an indirect free kick.

15 THROW-IN

A throw-in is taken along the sideline at the point where the ball went out of play. Originally designed to get the ball back in play as quickly as possible, the throw-in has developed into an effective attacking technique.

The ball must be thrown into play with both hands, from behind and over the head. The thrower must face the Field Of Play and as the ball is released, part of each foot must be on the ground on, or behind, the sideline.

If these rules are broken, or the thrower attempts to gain an unfair advantage by moving along the sideline, the throw-in will be given to the opposing team.

A goal cannot be scored direct from a throw-in, and the thrower may not touch the ball again until it has been touched by another player.

Some players have developed the skill of throwing the ball long distances, gaining their team vital tactical advantages, especially if the throw-in is awarded close to their opponents' penalty area.

For the throw-in, the throwing player must have both feet on or behind the sideline, and at least a part of both feet must remain in contact with the ground during the throw. Both hands, placed either side of the ball (or behind it in the case of a long throw, see pages 42–43), must be used for the throw-in.

16 GOAL KICK

Goal kicks are awarded to the defending team when the ball crosses their goal line outside the goal after having been last touched by an opponent. The ball is put back into play by a kick from the goal area.

Although the goalkeeper generally takes the goal kick, it may be taken by any other player in the team. The ball must be kicked outside the penalty area, although a short goal kick, to a defender standing outside the penalty area, is intended to retain possession and set up an attack. A long goal kick, especially in a following high wind, can be very effective because forwards cannot be offside on a goal kick.

A goal cannot be scored direct from a goal kick. If this happens the game is restarted with a goal kick to the opposing team, or a corner if the ball blows into the kicker's net.

The corner kick must be taken from within the quarter circle, so the ball at position B will not be allowed.

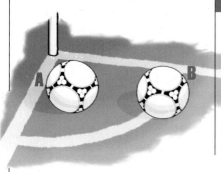

17 CORNER KICK

A corner kick is awarded to the attacking team if the ball crosses the goal line, either in the air or on the ground, having last been played by a member of the defending team. It is taken from the quarter circle by the corner flag on the appropriate side of the field. The flag must not be removed to take the kick. Opponents must stand at least ten yards away from the ball until it has been kicked. The kicker must not play the ball again until it has been touched by another player. Unlike an indirect free kick, a goal can be scored direct from a corner kick.

Skills and Techniques

TO be a soccer success, you need a combination of natural skill and dedication to constantly improve your techniques. You need to master the basic skills of the game, and must be able to control the ball, pass it to a teammate, shoot with either foot, head the ball and tackle opponents when necessary—in fact, develop a good balance of skills relating to the position you play. You will also need the vision to read games and playing situations. One thing's for sure, no matter if you are an international star, or whether you play for fun, you can never learn enough about the game.

(1) KICKING THE BALL

BEING able to kick the ball correctly is the game's most important basic skill to master. You need to have total control over the ball to insure it goes where you want it to, at the right pace.

Any part of the foot can be used to kick the ball (except the toes—it's difficult to control the ball with this part of the foot). Most players can kick a stationary ball quite easily, but you need to concentrate and practice all the different kicking techniques to be able to take corner kicks, free kicks and to pass, cross and shoot properly during a game.

Holland's Dennis Bergkamp (7) shoots for goal against Denmark.

The pass with inside of the foot

The inside of your foot is the area from your heel to big toe. This kicking area is used for short, accurate, low passes of up to 20 yards. This is the easiest way of passing the ball to a teammate because such a large area of foot is used.

Place the non-kicking foot alongside the ball and keep it pointed in the direction you want the ball to go. Keep your head down and eyes over the ball as you prepare to kick it. Raise your kicking foot two to three inches off the ground, turning it out almost at right angles. Keeping the ankle firm, bring your foot back and strike the ball firmly in the center. Follow through with your kicking foot to guide the ball in the direction you want it to go.

England's Chris Waddle and Romania's World Cup star Gheorghe Hagi are superb passers of the ball over short or long distances. You may recall Hagi's defense-splitting pass two minutes from the end of Romania's 1994 World Cup quarter-final tie against Sweden.

The score was 1–0 Sweden when Hagi's pass into the penalty box was met by Florin Raducioiu, who made no mistake from close range. That took the game into overtime, and Sweden won 5–4 on penalty kicks.

The pass with the outside of the foot

The outside of the foot is the flat area from the ankle to the end of the little toe. It's difficult to kick the ball straight using this area, so it is used mainly by the more experienced players to curl, or bend the ball in flight. The knee and kicking foot are turned inward and the outside front of the foot makes contact with the ball. Raise the kicking foot off the ground slightly and strike the center of the ball. This skill is useful when faced with an opponent who moves in to challenge you, just flick the ball away to one side to a teammate, or bend it around your challenger.

Kicking the ball with the outside of the foot is perfect for swerving passes or shots.

To insure a powerful and accurate lofted kick use the instep of the foot, strike beneath the ball and use a full follow-through.

The lofted kick

The instep of the foot is used for long distance passes over the heads of opponents, crossing the ball into the the area or corner kicks. To make the kick, lean backward with the supporting foot to the side of and slightly behind the ball. Once in position, strike beneath the ball to give you the necessary lift and follow through with a full leg swing.

Soccer Practice

Learn accuracy by kicking a ball against a wall which has been randomly marked out with numbered targets. Start off by aiming for target box 1. If you hit it go for box 2 and so on. You can play this on your own or with several players. When you miss the target, it is another player's turn. Every time it's your turn aim for the target you missed last time. After a while you can move further and further back and shoot from different angles.

Set up two cones (or similar objects) a small distance apart. Aim to kick the ball between the cones to a friend, who kicks the ball back.

Split your team into two lines on either side of a goal. Have one player from each group throw the ball at varying angles in for each player in turn to trap and then kick toward goal.

Stand between two players who are about 30 yards apart. As they lob the ball over your head, attempt to head it away. If you're successful, change places with one of the kickers. As your heading ability improves, try using two footballs.

In a marked area, players at each end bend the ball around a defender who is positioned in the middle.

The chip shot

If performed correctly this is one of the most dangerous and rewarding attacking kicks in the game. The "chip shot" can be used to score goals by lifting the ball over the goalkeeper's head if he has strayed too far off his line, open up the tightest defenses to put a teammate in a good attacking position, and to clear the ball if under pressure.

To play a chip shot you put your kicking foot and instep under the ball and flick your ankle. There should a short backlift of the leg and hardly any follow-through. This causes the ball to rise steeply.

The volley: note how the player swivels on the non-kicking foot and uses the instep of the other foot to strike the ball. Fine judgment of the ball's flight and pace is essential. The kick is made before the ball hits the ground.

The half-volley requires the same concentration and judgment as the volley, but the ball is struck after hitting the ground. Again, the instep should be the striking area to insure power and to control the low trajectory.

With a stabbing movement, strike the ball on its underside for the chip shot. A ball rolling toward you is easier to chip accurately than a stationary one.

The volley and half-volley

One of the most spectacular sights in soccer is a goal being scored by a player striking the ball on the volley from long range. "On the Volley" means to kick the ball while it is still in the air from a pass or a rebound. France's controversial superstar Eric Cantona practices this kick every day during training and has delighted fans with several goals scored on the volley. Timing and concentration are vital. To give the kick power the instep part of the foot should be used.

Keep your eyes firmly on the ball and try to judge its line of flight and pace. Leaning back away from the ball, balance on your non-kicking foot, swivel your body and strike the ball before it hits the ground. The toes should be pointed down to give maximum power. Remember to follow through with the kicking leg.

The half-volley is when you kick the ball just after it has hit the ground. Like the volley, the half-volley requires full concentration and the flight of the ball must be perfectly judged. Place your non-kicking foot close to the spot where you estimate the ball will bounce. As the ball hits the ground swing your kicking-foot through to make contact with the bouncing ball using the instep. Follow through keeping the kicking foot pointing downward and forward to keep the ball low and give it more power.

Unorthodox kicks

Overhead kicks can be used to catch goalkeepers by surprise, or to get yourself out of trouble on defense. If the kick comes off and a goal is scored you are a hero. If it doesn't you can be left flat on your back out of the action and looking like a clown.

As the ball comes over, your kicking foot should be at full stretch, with your toes reaching for it. Impact with the ball should be made with the flat of the foot on the laces, with your toes pointed toward your instep. Bend the knee of the non-kicking leg to insure your body leans backward. Bend your elbows and spread your hands to break your fall.

Wales's international striker Mark Hughes is an expert at the overhead kick (which is also a type of volley).

A swerving or curved pass can be used to make an inswinging corner kick, or to swerve the ball around a defensive wall. You can use either the inside or outside of the foot. When you strike the left side of the ball with your foot it curves to the right. Alternatively, striking the right side of the ball makes it curve to the left. Leaning your body over the ball will help gain greater control.

The back-heel

This can be used effectively to fake an opponent. When challenged you can deceive your opponent into thinking you are going to dribble the ball past him, but suddenly stop, step over the ball and back-heel it to a teammate. This move can leave your opponent stranded. But never attempt a back-heel in front of your own goal.

When back-heeling a ball, the supporting leg should be close to the ball. Strike the center of the ball with the back of the heel to provide power and accuracy to the shot, A slower, but more accurate method of back-heeling is to use the sole of the shoe to stop the ball before making contact. Only use this method if you have plenty of time.

The overhead kick is certainly the most visually exciting of the unorthodox kicks, requiring almost a somersault. Make sure that your elbows are bent and hands outstretched to break your fall.

INSET: the back-heel kick can be used to deceive opponents. Step over the ball you are dribbling, stop suddenly and use the heel to kick the ball back to a teammate in position.

② SHOOTING

THE objective of all soccer games is to score more goals than your opponents. Good goal scorers are essential to every team, that's why top strikers like Eric Wynalda are among soccer's most wanted men and are worth a fortune in today's transfer market. Wynalda is the most famous American playing in Germany today.

Although the goal scorer is generally the hero, the build-up to a goal requires teamwork, keeping possession of the ball, building up an attack and opening up defenses to create space in front of goal for the strikers to finish. Many strikers are natural, goal-hungry predators who rely on pure instinct. Nothing is more important to them than seeing the back of the net bulge.

Confidence, pace, height, control and body strength are a striker's vital assets. They also need to be brave to take the knocks that occur in the penalty area. England striker Alan Shearer and Germany's Jürgen Klinsmann are classic examples of the all-around, all-action striker. They have the ability to use all their skills and power while under pressure.

Goal scorers should have a sixth sense of where the goal is so they can shoot from any angle or distance without looking up. Hesitate on the ball, even for a split-second and a good scoring chance is often lost. The golden rule of shooting is always to hit the target and force the goalkeeper into making a save. Power and accuracy are needed to beat the goalkeeper, but don't always rely on sheer force, because even the fiercest of shots can be saved by a keeper's outstretched leg, arm or foot. Remember a goalkeeper also has instincts... for stopping the ball.

Goals can be scored by a number of different kicks, including gentle taps, chips, volleys or curling shots around the goalkeeper. These techniques and skills have been covered on pages 20–23. Goals can also be scored by putting pressure on defenders and goalkeepers in the penalty area and seizing any opportunity to knock the ball into the net.

Basic techniques

Your team may create many goal scoring opportunities in a game, but fail to take advantage of any of them and lose. To make sure you grab as many chances as possible you must practice shooting with moving balls because that is what happens in games.

Shooting covers several kicking and passing techniques that have been explained on pages 20–23. The art of good shooting is to strike a balance between control, accuracy and power... and to be able to kick with either foot!

When shooting, position your

Balance, control, accuracy and power—the perfect shooting technique, as shown by Dunga of Brazil.

supporting foot alongside the ball with toes pointing in the direction you want it to go. With eyes firmly on the ball, keep your head and shoulders over the ball, using your arms for balance. Swing back the kicking leg with toes pointed outward and then strike the ball in the middle with your instep. The kicking knee should be over the ball at the moment of impact to keep the shot low. With your head down and toes tensed and pointed, follow through with the kicking leg adding power from the knee. If the ball has been struck with great power the force should lift your body off the ground.

If the ball is moving away from you as you are about to shoot, place your kicking foot ahead of it and strike with your toes pointed and tensed.

Shooting from a distance

To shoot from long range you need to be able to kick with great power and be aware of the situation around you. If a teammate is in a better position to score you should consider passing the ball. Also be aware of where the goalkeeper is positioned. A surprise shot from outside the area could catch him and the opposing

defenders off guard.

For maximum power, the non-kicking foot should be alongside the

---

Soccer Practice

Use a wall to practice your shooting and ball control. Mark out targets and use both feet when kicking. Start by standing four to five yards from the wall, gradually increasing the distance between you and the wall. See how many times you can hit the target in a minute.

Get two players to stand on either side of the penalty area and take turns firing balls towards the penalty-spot at all angles and heights for a third player to run on to and kick while it is moving. If no goalkeeper is available, shoot at a wall.

During five-a-side games or training, occasionally try not to use your good foot. If you are naturally right-footed, always get the ball on your left. Or play with a soccer shoe on your weak foot and a softer training shoe on your strong foot.

Practice volleying by getting a friend to throw balls towards the penalty spot for you to strike before they hit the ground. When you have improved get another player to act as a defender and run from behind you and try to get the ball before you can kick it. This will get you used to being under pressure and help speed up your reactions.

For chip shots, place a number of balls on the edge of the penalty area and see how many times you can hit the crossbar with them.

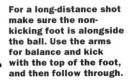

For a long-distance shot make sure the non-kicking foot is alongside the ball. Use the arms for balance and kick with the top of the foot, and then follow through.

Attacker (A) shoots for a goal. If the shot is pushed out by the goalkeeper or strikes the far post the ball could rebound to attackers (B) or (C).

Brazil's Bebeto side-foots to score from close range against the USA in World Cup '94

ball with your head over the ball. Arms should be outstretched to the side for balance. The ball should be struck with the top of the foot with the toe of the kicking foot kept down. Remember, keep your eyes on the ball and follow through with the kicking leg after striking the ball.

Your head must be down over the ball in order to keep the shot close to the ground. Low shots, particularly when aimed at the corners of the goal, are more difficult for the goalkeeper to deal with than high shots directed just under the crossbar.

The great Dutch international star Ronald Koeman is famous for his long-rage shooting. It was his tremendous, thunderous 25-yard drive from a free kick that won the European Cup for Barcelona against Sampdoria at Wembley in 1992. Another long-range expert is Brazil's Branco.

Shooting from close range

England's former striker Gary Lineker scored many goals by pure

When shooting from the edge of the penalty area, always aim just inside the far post.

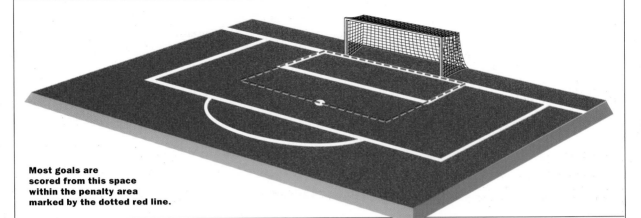

Most goals are scored from this space within the penalty area marked by the dotted red line.

instinct and reflex action from inside the six-yard box. Anticipation and accuracy are more important than blasting from close range. Always be on the lookout for rebounds—stay alert and be ready to pounce to gently tap, or side-foot, the ball into the net.

Positioning in the penalty area

Most goals are scored in an area that extends from the six-yard box to the penalty spot. The best area for scoring goals is seen by drawing a line from the goalposts to the edge of the penalty area, as shown in the diagram below. Inside the blue area you should pass the ball to a teammate who might be in a better position. Inside the red area, shoot for goal!

While play is inside the penalty area, you should be aware of the play around you and get into a position to snap up balls that have rebounded off posts, defenders' legs or been parried by the goalkeeper. If a shot misses the target and flies across the goal, a player running in on the far post will have a good chance of reaching it and scoring.

Way-To-Play Tips

Eyes on the ball
It's important to keep your eyes firmly on the ball when making impact with it. Just before you strike look up to see where the goalkeeper is. You can take advantage of a badly-positioned goalkeeper.

Don't be afraid to miss
When shooting from long range don't be afraid of missing. If you are nervous you will lack confidence which will probably affect your accuracy.

Don't always aim for the center of the goal. Pick a target such as the far post, or corner of the goal – vulnerable spots for goalkeepers.

Always follow up shots and make sure the ball has crossed the line if you are in any doubt.

Never change your mind as you prepare to shoot. He who hesitates loses.

Train and practice shooting with a recognized goalkeeper if possible. You won't learn anything, or get any real benefit out of taking shots at a field player who knows very little about stopping the ball.

- - - - **Go for a goal in this area.**
- - - - **Inside this area pass the ball.**

IF you are unable to trap or control a soccer ball you cannot play the game well, so it's a vital skill to learn and master. You must be able to stop the ball dead and bring it under control, often under pressure in a crowded area of the field.

A good first touch of the ball gives you the space and time to make the next move and pass to a teammate, take opponents on, or shoot for goal. It also enables you to shield the ball with your body to hold off a challenge until you are able to make a positive move. If you cannot trap the ball, opponents will find it easy to mark you tightly and will quickly take the ball from you when you lose control.

Basic technique

Whichever part of the body is used to control or trap the ball, the basic technique is the same. Keep your eyes firmly on the ball and get your body into the line of flight so you are perfectly balanced and ready to take it in your stride. At the moment of impact, relax whichever part of the body you are using to control the ball. This movement acts as a cushion and slows down the ball, making it easier to control. A tensed leg, foot, chest or head acts as a firm barrier and the ball will bounce away from you.

Be positive and aware of how you are going to trap the ball and position your body accordingly, especially if you are being tightly marked by an opponent.

Trapping the ball with the inside of the foot

Keep your eyes on the ball, with your balancing foot firmly on the ground. Use the raised foot making contact with the ball to absorb, or cushion, its power by pulling it back slightly at the moment of impact. After it hits the leg the ball should drop to the ground,

making it easy to control with the inside of your foot. You are then ready to move away with the ball, or pass to a teammate.

The trapping foot should be relaxed to cushion the ball. The more pace you can take off the ball, the easier it

Trapping the ball with the inside of the foot (top) and the outside (bottom).

is to control. Keep your balance so that you can move quickly away with the ball. Timing is also important, or the ball could bounce away from you.

Trapping with the outside of the foot

To trap the ball with the outside of your foot, lean your body toward the ball's flight. At the moment of impact the foot should be relaxed and the knee slightly bent to cushion and slow down the ball's pace. If you are about to be challenged, keep your supporting leg between the ball and your opponent. This helps to retain your balance and shield the ball from a challenger.

You should now be ideally placed to pass to a team-mate, or go around an opponent. If you are being marked, your opponent will find it difficult to tackle and get the ball from you without committing a foul.

Chest traps

When a high ball is falling, a player may not be in a position to wait for it to reach the ground before trapping and getting it under control. So, using the chest is the answer. Often high balls crossed into the penalty area have to be controlled at chest height before a striker is in a position to shoot for goal.

Experienced defenders also deflect balls away from danger by turning their chest as the ball hits it—but you should always try to head the ball clear.

You must keep your eyes on the ball, get your body in line with the flight as it comes toward you and correct your balance by using your arms. Watching the ball closely as it continues to drop, bend your knees slightly and extend your arms. You should be up on your toes and leaning back slightly as the ball makes contact with your chest. Try to cushion the impact by relaxing your chest muscles. Lean your head over the ball as it falls to your feet.

Great defenders such as Steve Bruce, captain of the 1994 English Premier League Champions, Manchester United, have perfected the chest trap and often use it to deflect the ball to safety. In the

In a chest trap, the ball's impact is cushioned by leaning back and relaxing the chest muscles to bring the ball under control.

If the ball is falling towards you at an awkward angle, use the thigh trap to stop it and bring it under control.

Way-To-Play Tips

Cushion control
You can gain control of the ball more quickly and more effectively by taking the pace off it. As the ball hits your legs or chest, relax the muscles, bending your legs slightly on impact to cushion it.

One touch
Remember to control the ball with your first touch, and to pass or to take opponents on or shoot for goal with your second. This way you will not give an opponent the opportunity to tackle you.

European Cup-Winners' Cup Final against Barcelona in 1991, Steve contributed to United's victory by clearing the danger on several occasions by pushing the ball away with his chest. He does this by tensing his chest at the moment of impact and twisting his body from the hips to send the ball in the direction he wants.

Thigh traps

The thigh is often used to control a ball that's dropping toward you at an awkward height when you are on the move. It can also be used to push the ball into the air to allow you to volley it with the other leg. Alternatively, thigh control makes the ball drop to the feet quicker than the chest trap. Turn your body toward the ball, relax the thigh muscles and allow it to hit your thigh. Make sure your supporting leg is slightly bent. Let the ball drop to your feet ready to pass, or turn quickly to lose your marker.

Soccer Practice

Make a triangle using three players. Trap and pass the ball between you. Keep the ball moving and pass over longer distances as you improve your control.

A simple exercise on your own is to throw a ball into the air and trap it as it falls to the ground, using the inside of your foot.

One player passes to you when you're positioned inside the center circle. Trap the ball while being challenged by a third player and try to pass back to the first player, who runs around the edge of the center circle. Take it in turns to change position.

Find two walls at right angles. Kick the ball against one wall and when it comes back trap and hit it against the other wall. Use your feet and head in five- to ten-minute turns. Increase the times when you improve.

ONE of the most exciting sights in the game is to see a player go on a run and dribble the ball past several opponents, while keeping it under close control. The player weaves one way, then the other, evading tackle after tackle before using his pace to leave opponents stranded.

You might recall Diego Maradona's second goal for Argentina in the 1986 World Cup quarter-finals when he darted through the heart of England's defense—the ball appeared to be glued to his foot! Italy's World Cup star Roberto Baggio also possesses all the attributes needed to be a superb attacking player, and is a prime example for all young players to watch at every opportunity and to try to emulate.

But remember, soccer is a team game. Dribbling past three or four defenders and then losing the ball to a

Italy's Roberto Baggio is well balanced as he sprints into space with the ball.

fifth who starts a dangerous counter-attack is no good for your team. Dribbling and running with the ball are most effective on the wings, especially against tight defenses.

Once near the sideline you can cross the ball to teammates positioned in front of goal. Defenders forced into the tackle can often be left stranded, or have to concede a corner.

To have good dribbling skills you need ball control, balance and pace, and quick reactions in one-on-one situations. Running with the ball to get away from opponents and move into space requires pace, close control and an awareness of the players around you. While running with the ball look around to spot opponents about to challenge, or teammates who are in good positions to receive a pass.

Basic technique

To dribble a ball well you must think of it as part of your foot. Lean over the ball and keep it within comfortable, controllable distance, close enough to allow you to move away or change direction if you are challenged. Notice how your opponent is standing. Flat-footed players instead of on their toes will be slow off the mark when challenging or chasing you.

When running with the ball, push it slightly ahead of you. The faster you run the further you can push the ball. Try to combine pace and balance with a body swerve and a dip of the shoulder to confuse your opponent as to the direction you are going.

Keeping the ball on the blindside

If you're in possession of the ball and being closely marked you may often have to move forward, or (more often than not) hold on to the ball until you're in a better position to release it. You will have to protect, or shield, the ball by keeping your body between it and the opponent. This prevents the opponent from seeing or reaching the ball.

With head leaned forward, put your weight on the non-kicking foot. Hold your arms out slightly behind your body. This helps your balance and makes it difficult for your opponent to tackle.

Run with the ball as the opponent

moves in to tackle from the side. As the challenge comes from the left, control the ball with the outside of your right foot, or the outside of your left foot if challenged from the right

Twist and turn to keep your back to your opponent and then use a body swerve, or dummy to move away with the ball on his blind side.

Change of pace

Move toward an opponent at your normal speed but when close to him drop a shoulder and veer away slightly, stepping up the pace until you are sprinting away with the ball.

If an opponent runs alongside you, slow down and then suddenly pick up the pace again to leave him stranded. You can also catch opponents wrong-footed by pretending to stop the ball with the sole of a foot and then dragging it along in the same direction, accelerating away.

Swerving

This is a simple way to wrong-foot a defender. Drop a shoulder and look as if you intend to go off in one direction, for example to the right. As your opponent moves to the right to cover, swerve your body past on the left. If you carry this out correctly, the defender will be caught off balance and won't recover in time to challenge.

Feinting

One of the simplest (but often the most impressive) ways of beating an opponent by catching him off balance is to pretend to play the ball in one direction, but play it the opposite way. As an opponent moves in to challenge, make a kicking motion, but in the last second check your kick. Use the same foot to drag or push the ball away in another direction.

A player feints to kick the ball really hard, but instead swivels on the standing foot and turns the ball with the inside of the playing foot behind the standing leg.

Another good dummy, or feint, is to run with the ball and pretend to push it along with the outside of the foot, but instead pass the foot over the ball and drag it forward with the

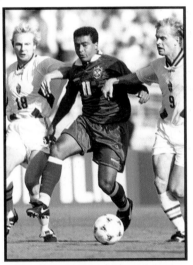

Brazil's Romario running with the ball displays both pace and close control

Way-To-Play Tips

Don't get mugged
Do not dribble the ball in your own penalty area. You could easily lose possession.

Speed is important, but so is close control. Regulate your pace to be sure you keep possession of the ball.

Do not use the same foot when dribbling. Juggle the ball from foot to foot, also varying your speed to keep opponents guessing.

Try not to get pushed out wide, or take on one opponent too many. Always look for the opportunity to catch out opponents by passing to a teammate.

Call a teammate by name as if you are going to pass. This diverts your opponent's attention long enough for you to take the ball past him.

Look up and be aware of the players around you.

inside of the other foot. Check your pace and then accelerate as you play the ball with the inside of your foot.

Evading a tackle

Be extremely careful when on the ball because a defender attempting to tackle you can, even accidentally, give you a very nasty injury if he kicks you. As he lunges for the ball make sure neither you nor the ball are in the way.

Soccer Practice

Set up a row of cones, garden sticks, or plastic bottles about six yards apart. Weave in and out of the cones with a ball, using the inside and outside of the foot. When you have reached the end of the obstacles, stop the ball with the sole of your shoe, turn and go in the other direction. Time yourself and try to beat your best time.

You can use this exercise on your own, or with a friend. If there are two of you, pass the ball to your partner once you have reached the end of the course. The partner plays the ball back to you so that you have to control it before setting off down the course again.

Five players acting as forwards stand in a position about 12–15 yards outside the penalty area. Each is confronted by a defender standing just inside the area. Each attacker then runs at their respective opponent trying to dribble past into the area and shoot for goal. After an agreed amount of time the defenders change places with the attackers.

ONCE you can control the ball you will need to learn about distribution—to keep possession by linking with teammates with good, accurate passes. This can be done using the head or feet, on the ground or in the air, over long and short distances. You can even use your hands. A throw-in is a pass, as is a throw-out by a goalkeeper.

Accurate passing of the ball is a skill. England's Paul Gascoigne at his best is a tremendous distributor of the ball, especially in tight situations. So are Germany's star Lothar Matthäus and Enzo Scifo of Belgium.

When you're about to pass the ball you must carefully consider a number of possibilities before releasing it. If the ball is struck too hard it will be difficult for the receiver to control it. If the ball is not struck hard enough it could fail to reach its target and be intercepted by an opponent. If the ball is kicked into space for a teammate to run on to, your team could lose possession.

It is also important to look up when you are about to release the ball to see exactly where your teammates and opponents are. Like Gascoigne, Matthäus and Scifo, good passes need control of the ball, accuracy, good balance and an awareness of the situation to ensure you don't give the ball away.

Basic technique

To pass accurately you have to be able to kick the ball well and with confidence, using the inside, outside or instep of your foot (or feet!). When passing, keep your eyes on the ball at the moment of impact, and use your arms for balance. Strike the ball in its middle for low passes. Strike it just below the center-line for long, lofted passes. Follow through with the kicking foot in a deliberate, smooth action and with the non-kicking foot pointed in the direction you want the ball to go.

The side-foot or push pass

This is the most common, and most accurate way of passing to a teammate along the ground over a short distance. Your non-kicking foot should be on the ground alongside the ball. Look at the teammate you are about to pass to, then strike the ball in the center with the inside of

Soccer Practice

Playing in twos is an excellent way to practice basic passing, and to perfect that all-important accuracy at speed. Here are some handy tips to train yourself:

Stand parallel to a teammate about four to five yards apart. Run up and down the field, keeping your distance and passing the ball to each other. Each pass is made slightly ahead of the receiver so he can take the ball and play it in his stride. The receiver controls the ball using the inside of his far foot and passes it back in the next stride with the same foot. Repeat the exercise over a ten minute spell, gradually increasing the distance between you and your partner.

A good training exercise for four or more players involves interpassing in a triangular formation. Three players (A, B and C) pass to each other in a triangle. The ball is passed between any one of them and (D), who is continuing on the move and returns the ball to any one of the three players. They should remain alert in anticipation of (D) making a pass. Switch positions around after a few minutes.

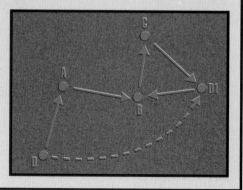

your foot, keeping your body over the ball. Swing through with a pendulum movement from the hip to complete the pass.

The long pass

As with the push pass, your non-kicking foot must be alongside the ball and pointing toward the player about to receive. Use your instep to make the ball rise in the air. Keeping your ankle firm, lift back the kicking foot with toes pointed toward the ground and aim to strike the ball below the center. As you strike the ball lean back and follow through to ensure it is hit with power.

The Wall Pass

When under pressure, or closely marked, you can use the wall pass, or return pass using the inside of your foot to a teammate who has moved away at an angle to you As he collects the ball you move away on the blind side of your marker and take a quick return pass in your stride, leaving him stranded. In a sense you have used your teammate as a wall to bounce the ball off. This is also known as the "one-two."

Running off the ball

There is no use passing the ball unless you have a teammate to pass it to. Successful moves and build-ups rely on unmarked players being in positions to receive the ball when they have run into space. They will then have time to control the ball and pass it on before being challenged. All good players have the vision to move into space to avoid being marked. Timing the run is vital. Move too soon and you could find yourself under heavy pressure when the pass is made.

Way-To-Play Tips

Pass and run
After delivering a pass to a teammate you should run into space to support him and be ready to take a return pass. Many teams base their game on this simple tactic.

Make it tough for defenders
Try to keep yourself between the defender and the ball when passing to make it difficult for him to challenge you.

On the move
Always be on the move into space when you haven't got the ball. You will be much more difficult to mark, and be in a position to receive a pass without being challenged.

Foot talk
Remember the instep is used to achieve power, the inside of the foot for accuracy and the outside of the foot to swerve the ball and catch your opponent off-guard. The stronger and straighter the follow-through, the greater the power and accuracy.

INSET shows the side-foot, or push pass, where the ball is struck in the center with the inside of the foot, directing it accurately toward a temmate.

Power and accuracy are vital to the long pass. Note how the player's non-kicking foot is placed alongside the ball to help the shot's aim. The ball is kicked just below its center to loft it; the follow-through provides the power.

FLUID PASSING scorching shooting and nifty ball control all look great but to achieve any of them, you have to have the ball! This is where the less glamorous but vital art of tackling comes in.

To win the ball you must tackle an opponent. A good tackle is a hard but fair challenge on the player with the ball. Like passing, shooting and dribbling, tackling requires skill and technique. Expert tacklers not only win the ball, but can set up a counter-attack. Italian international star Paolo Maldini is one of the world's top defenders. He's a very strong tackler but also a superb reader of the game. Once he's won the ball his distribution is world class. England star midfielder Paul Ince is also a brilliant winner and distributor of the ball. But tackling does not only concern defenders or ball-winning midfielders. Every player on the field, including the goalkeeper, should acquire and practice the art of winning the ball cleanly. There are three basic methods of tackling; the front block, the side block and the sliding tackle.

Basic technique

Keep your eyes on the ball and not your opponent, and use the side of your foot to make contact with the ball. Challenge for the ball when you are confident of winning it. Timing is vital to avoid missing the ball and striking your opponent. This will be called a foul by the referee.

So, be accurate, put the whole of your leg and weight into the tackle and go in with determination. Hesitation, or relaxing your body, could result in your opponent brushing you aside, or you could suffer a serious injury.

But certain methods of tackling are determined by a defender's position or attacking line of approach by an opponent.

The front block tackle

This is the strongest form of tackling against an opponent. It is used when two players going for the ball reach it at the same time—also known as going for a 50/50 ball. As your opponent tries to play the ball, go in close and

In a 50/50 ball situation, the front block tackle is the most powerful means of gaining possession. The inside of the foot is used to block the ball, and then scoop it away from the challenger. In all tackling situations, look at the ball, not at your opponent.

Use the side block tackle to take the ball off an opponent running in the same direction as yourself.

use the side of your foot to block the ball firmly. When you've made contact with the ball, make sure all your body weight is on the tackling leg. Leaning a shoulder toward your opponent adds strength to your challenge.

The side block tackle

You would use the side block tackle to take the ball off an opponent running in the same direction as yourself. When tackling an opponent from an angle, or side, you must put all your weight on the tackling leg, with your supporting leg slightly bent. As you make contact with the ball, turn and lean forward in the direction of the tackle.

The slide tackle

The aim of the sliding tackle is not so much to gain possession of the ball, but to deflect it away from your

The perfect slide tackle requires split-second timing. Here, Nicola Berti of Italy tackles Norway's Lars Bohinen during the 1994 World Cup.

Soccer Practice

Use a small field with four attackers against three defenders marking man-to-man, with the spare attacker allowed only to receive the ball from a back pass.

Mark out a small area ten yards square, or use the penalty area. Then, using three players, one tries to win the ball, while the other two pass it between them. Take turns being the attacker.

Stand as a pair facing each other one step from the ball. Both of you place your left foot slightly behind and to the side of the ball. Then, using the right foot, make a block tackle at the ball. Increase the power of the tackle and switch to the other foot after ten minutes.

One player runs down the field in a straight line with the ball. After five or six yards, another player runs in pursuit and attempts to gain possession of the ball with a fair slide tackle from behind, hooking the ball away with the attacking foot.

Play three-a-side games in which the players must beat an opponent before passing the ball. This encourages dribbling and tackling.

Set up two cones five or six yards apart. One player (A) stands between the cones, while two others (B and C) position themselves on either side, ten yards away. The two players (B and C) pass the ball to each other between the cones, while player (A) tries to intercept. This is good defensive training.

opponent to a teammate or safely out of play. This is a difficult tackling skill to perfect. To win the ball cleanly and not foul your opponent after totally committing yourself requires split-second timing. Try to go for the ball with your strongest leg, aiming your foot slightly in front of it. Keeping you eyes firmly on the ball, bend your supporting leg and slide on the knee and shin of this leg, putting your weight behind the tackling foot. A bent arm helps support the body when the tackling foot stretches to play the ball. After deflecting, or blocking the ball, withdraw your foot to avoid tripping your opponent. Watch Brazillian defender Marcio Santos in action. He performs the sliding tackle magnificently because his timing is perfect, and he generally comes away with the ball.

The back-heel tackle

Get close to the player you intend tackling so you are running side by side with each other. With eyes on the ball raise the foot of the tackling leg and block the ball with your heel. Do not swing the leg backward, but check as it makes contact with the ball transferring your weight to the tackling foot.

The shoulder charge

Maneuver yourself into position by running alongside the player you are about to challenge. In a slightly crouching position come shoulder to shoulder with your opponent. Make sure you only use your upper arm and shoulder when making contact and from the side, not behind.

When you touch put all your weight into the shoulder you are using and lean in with the supporting leg to give you balance. When your opponent is off balance, use the side of the foot to attack and win the ball.

INSET: The back-heel tackle is like a back-heel kick, but the aim is to block the ball. However, it is a dangerous tackle to try.

In the shoulder charge the challenge must be from the side, using only the upper arm and shoulder to make contact. The object is to unbalance your opponent so that you can use the side of the foot to capture the ball.

BELOW: Although the defender is going to get the ball in the tackle, the attacker will probably be brought down as he won't be able to lift his leg over the tackler. This should not be a foul, but it is a risky challenge.

Jockeying for position is a way of frustrating an opponent in possession of the ball and forcing him to make a mistake so that you can go in for a tackle.

Way-To-Play Tips

Perfect timing

Timing is essential. Go in hard, but take the ball cleanly. A mistimed tackle can result in a foul and a free kick or penalty kick being awarded against you as well as being shown a yellow or red card.

Confidence and determination

Always believe you are going to win the ball. Go in half-heartedly and you'll be pushed aside, or risk injury.

Tackle in training

Don't hold off tackling during training or five-a-side games. Some teams do this to avoid injuries. But you play as you train. If you stop tackling in training defenders can develop a bad habit of holding off, or hesitating during a game, while forwards can get a false sense of security when in possession.

Stand-up

Don't dive in when tackling. Stay on your feet. You can't tackle effectively on the ground.

Side on

Presenting most of your body to an opponent you are about to tackle, the frontal stance, is the best method to adopt when you are a young player. But when you gain experience, the diagonal stance to an opponent will force him to move in other directions and so be less confident on the ball.

Jockeying for position

You can stop an opponent in possession by "jockeying," or closing the player down and setting him up for the tackle. When your opponent has the ball under control approach, keeping your eyes on the ball. As he moves toward you, back off slowly, giving him as little space as possible in which to play the ball, or increase his pace. Keep your eyes on the ball and wait until he makes a mistake or turns. Some players are uncomfortable if they keep the ball too long. They get frustrated and take risks. When you feel confident of getting the ball, go firmly into the tackle. It is important to remain patient and stay on your feet.

HEADING the ball is a vital facet of the game, but one of the most difficult skills to master. The most common fault among youngsters when learning to head a soccer ball is fear—they are afraid of not connecting with the ball properly and getting hurt.

Because heading is a not a natural action, you may reflexively close your eyes when heading the ball. As a result you make contact with the top of the head and not with your forehead. Closing the eyes when an object gets near is a natural reflex action and nothing to be ashamed of. But conquering it is essential if you want to be a better player.

So, as with all techniques covered in this book, it is a vital that you practice the skill until you are comfortable heading the ball. Although the technique of heading the ball is basically the same, there are four distinct types of header: attacking; defensive; glancing; and cushion (or head trap).

Basic technique

Whichever type of header you perform, they all require perfect timing and confidence. Apart from the glancing header, the ball should be met with the forehead. This is the strongest part of the skull and is much harder and tougher than a soccer ball. By using your forehead, the eyes can follow the ball right to the moment of impact.

Concentrate and keep your eyes on the ball as it drops toward you, thinking about where you want the ball to go. Just before contact with the ball tense your neck muscles and move your head slightly back. Imagine you have a target painted on your forehead, and aim to meet the ball in the bulls eye.

When you make contact with the ball, thrust your forehead forward sharply. Follow through with your body, bending your elbows back to help add more power to the header. This action gives the ball a great deal of impetus and if your technique is good, you'll also avoid getting hurt.

Belgium's Enzo Scifo (10) heads the ball away from Holland's Bryan Roy.

Soccer Practice

In threes: The players stand in a triangular formation about five yards apart. A throws the ball to B, who heads the ball on to (C). (C) fields the ball, throws it to (A) who heads it to (B), and so on...

In pairs: Stand 12 yards apart. Throw the ball so that your partner can make a standing jump to head it back.

In pairs: Stand 15 yards apart. Throw the ball so that your partner can run forward and jump to head it back.

Heading Volley Ball

Two teams, six-a-side, compete in heading the ball over a net (seven feet high) without letting the ball touch the ground. The ball is served by a player from the base-line of the court, striking it with his hand to send it over the net. The ball is then headed back and forth over the net. If it drops to the ground, fails to go over the net, or goes out of play, the service or the point is lost to the other side. This game is well suited to indoor arenas.

For a cushion header, you don't need to nod the ball as powerfully, but follow the same procedure up until the moment of contact. If you have to jump for the ball it is better to try and run forward to meet it, taking off on one foot while you are running. This gives you greater height than a standing jump with both feet.

When you do jump, remember to keep your arms down. You don't need to use your elbows for leverage, and jumping at an opponent is a foul.

Attacking headers

The aim of the attacking header is to meet the ball powerfully with the forehead to create havoc in an opposing penalty area, and hopefully beat the defense and goalkeeper.

This header, like a shot at goal, should be aimed low. Goalkeepers have most difficulty going down low to make a save. Remember, an attacking header is likely to be made from a cross into the area. The keeper may already have attempted to go up to meet the cross so his positioning and balance may not be quite right—this gives you a distinct advantage. So remember that the key to the attacking header is heading the ball down.

England captain David Platt has often won games by timing his runs to arrive late in the penalty area and score with an attacking header.

Germany's World Cup star Rudi Völler is also a great exponent of the attacking header.

Heading for goal

This may seems obvious, but it is worth remembering that if you head the ball downward, you will be

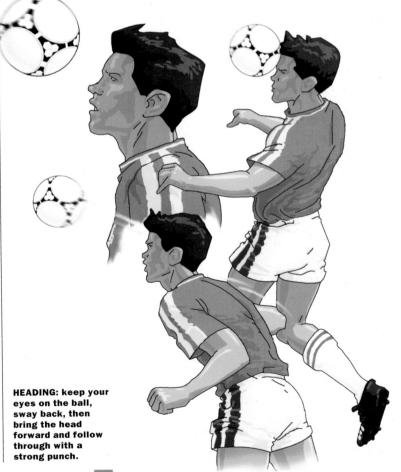

HEADING: keep your eyes on the ball, sway back, then bring the head forward and follow through with a strong punch.

Mark Hughes attacks the ball with his head, achieving great power and accuracy.

head a low cross which cannot be reached with a foot. They are very hard to defend against. A diving header can also be used defensively to protect your goal, or clear your line.

As with headers, the basic technique remains the same, but there are three things to stress:
(1) throw your arms out in front, below the height of your shoulders, to add power to your dive;
(2) make contact with your forehead and not the top of the head;
(3) bend your knees and relax your arms to help soften your fall.

Defensive headers

Defenders must be able to head the ball powerfully and over a long distance upfield when the team is under pressure. They must also be strong enough to attack the ball and reach it before an opponent in a crowded penalty area and clear the danger.

When heading for defense don't wait for the ball to drop, attack it as it arrives, jumping and striking the ball in the middle of your forehead. Don't worry about opponents. Pay too much attention to them, rather than the ball, and you'll lose concentration.

Jumping for the ball

To gain height, lean forward as you jump. Before you head the ball, arch your back and flex your neck and shoulder muscles. When you are in the air try to hit the ball at the highest point you can reach. Hammer your head and neck forward in one movement to add power to your header. Make contact with the center of the ball.

extremely unlucky if your effort goes over the crossbar. This is the main reason that defenders head up while attackers head down.

The vast majority of headers on goal come either from crosses or other glanced headers, which are discussed later. This frequently means that the penalty area is likely to be quite crowded, so getting into position becomes even more important. When you decide to go for the ball, be aware of the position of your opponents, the goalkeeper, and most importantly, the goal.

If you are outside the penalty area,

pick out the line of flight of the ball, run in, jump and make contact with the ball at the point where you estimate it will arrive in front of goal.

When heading for goal from crosses, head the ball back in the direction from which it came, aiming for the near post. The goalkeeper may be screened or out of position. Headers aimed down are much more accurate than balls headed in the air.

Diving headers

Often diving headers result in spectacular goals when an attacking player decides to dive full length to

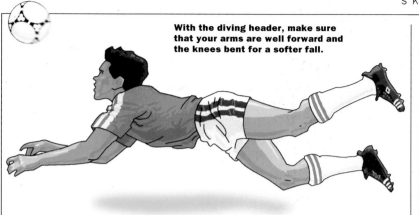

With the diving header, make sure that your arms are well forward and the knees bent for a softer fall.

Eye on the ball

Remember, once you have decided to go for a header don't change your mind! Attack the ball by getting in front of your opponent. Watch the ball right up to the moment of impact.

Don't duck

Do not head the ball if it is below your waist (except for diving headers) or you might get kicked in the face by an opponent.

Time your jumps

Good heading usually involves jumping off the ground. This will help you with high balls and gives you a big advantage over your opponents.

Backward danger

Avoid heading the ball when you are running backward. In this position you will not be able to jump for the ball, or generate enough power or control over your header.

Timing the jump is essential if you are to get the required power and height into the jump. Even a short run and single-foot take off will give you greater height than you can achieve from a standing jump with both feet.

If you're defending, covering an opponent from behind, and you need to jump vertically to go for a high ball, you should stand slightly away from the player you're marking so you have the space to run forward when making a jump for the ball. This prevents you from making bodily contact with your opponent, which is foul play.

The glancing header

For a glancing header, or "flick-on," the forehead is used to deflect the ball away in different directions. You can use the force of the ball as you make contact to redirect it away from an opponent, or toward goal. The forehead acts as a block, or gliding surface, off which to bounce the ball.

When you've made contact with the ball, twist your head and body in the direction you wish it to go. The harder you strike a ball, the more power and pace your glancing header will have. This can prove decisive in front of goal.

With the glancing header, also referred to as the "flick-on," use your head and body to glance the ball in the desired direction.

BASICALLY, a throw-in is a method of restarting play. However, in the modern game it can be used as a tactical weapon that could lead to a goal being scored, so it is an important skill to get right.

Taking a throw-in should be easy, especially as there are 20–40 awarded during every game. But it's amazing how many people get it wrong, commit a foul throw, and give the advantage to the opposition.

You should select certain players in your team to take the throw-ins when the ball goes out of play. Not being clear about who is going to take throw-ins can lead to the loss of vital seconds (in which time the opposition can regroup). You don't want to see teammates arguing among themselves as to who is going to take a throw-in. And you don't want to have a team confused because no one steps forward to take the throw.

Players receiving the ball from a throw-in should always move around. Keep moving to create space making you much more difficult to mark and close down.

The player throwing the ball in should select a teammate to throw the ball to, or throw the ball into space for him to run on to. Don't just throw the ball in the general direction of a teammate. Make sure he knows what your intentions are.

Remember, when in an attacking position the player receiving the ball cannot be offside from a throw-in.

Basic technique

The player taking the throw-in must stand with both feet on or behind the sideline at the point where the ball went out of play. Both hands must be on the ball, which is thrown from behind and over the head. You may raise your heels, but must have part of each foot firmly on the ground. When throwing the ball it is advisable to stand just behind the sideline to avoid putting one, or both, feet on to the Field Of Play.

The long throw

This can be a useful attacking option anywhere within 30 yards of your opponent's penalty area, and can be as effective as a corner kick. The long throw is used prominently in the British game. In the rest of the world—and at international level—teams usually rely on the short, quick throw.

Wimbledon and Wales defender Vinny Jones, often criticized for his

Soccer Practice

In pairs: one player sits down, the other stands up five yards away. The standing player throws the ball to the sitting player who catches it and throws it back from behind the head.

In pairs: stand with feet astride, ten yards apart. Throw a ball overhead to each other. After a few minutes do the same but with one foot forward. This will enable you to put more pace on the ball.

In pairs: your partner throws a ball to you. Control it with your head, chest or feet before kicking it back. If the ball bounces before reaching the partner, switch roles.

Safety in the defensive third of the field is vital. With his teammates marked, full back (A) has room to clear the throw-in from player (B).

"over-enthusiastic tackling," is an expert at the long throw into opponents' danger areas to teammates with height advantage.

For long throws, the hands should be placed behind the ball (not on the

In the long throw-in, the hands should be placed behind the ball to provide more power. Lean well back with one leg extended behind the throw, but still insuring both feet remain on the ground and on or behind the sideline.

Way-To-Play Tips

Don't let the ball bounce
Throw the ball to the receiver's head, chest or feet. Don't throw it in front of him. If the ball bounces it will be more difficult to control and he could lose it to an opponent.

Dummy runs
If you are about to receive the ball from a throw-in, move as if you are going to run in one direction, but then quickly switch and move in another. Your marker will be caught off-guard and you'll create extra space to receive the ball from the thrower.

Concentrate
Always concentrate on the basics. Lifting a foot, or failing to take the ball behind the head will result in a foul throw. Why make it easy for the opposition?

Quick return
You can retain possession if the receiver plays the ball straight back to the player who has just taken the throw-in.

Kick-ins
One experiment being carried out in some countries (Belgium and Hungary are two) is the kick-in. As its name suggests, players kick the ball back into play instead of throwing it in. In England, kick-ins are being used in the Diadora League for the 1994-95 season. The U.S. may experiment with kick-ins in some leagues soon.

side as for a normal throw-in) to give it extra power, height and distance. Lean back as far as you can, remembering to keep both feet on the ground behind the sideline, lifting your heels off the ground. Tense your stomach muscles and heave your body forward, swinging the arms powerfully over your head. With a final flick of the fingers, propel the ball high into the danger zone.

The long throw-in can also be used by defenders to throw it back to their goalkeeper, or down the sideline for an attacking teammate to run on to.

Strong stomach muscles and powerful shoulders are essential to achieve an effective long throw-in.

The short, quick throw-in

A short throw-in taken quickly can be just as effective as a long throw. These are used to get the ball back into play, to keep possession, set up attacking opportunities and catch opponents off guard.

THERE'S an old saying in the game that "you have to be crazy to be a goalkeeper." True or not, you certainly do need to be a different character from the rest of the team.

Goalkeeping is a highly specialized role. This is the most important member of the team, playing in the most demanding and difficult position of all, requiring extra skills and abilities than any outfield player.

They are under constant pressure to play well because the slightest mistake can be cruelly punished and result in a goal being scored, or even worse, defeat. Field players can afford to have an off day and make the occasional mistake. But not goalkeepers.

Good goalkeeping is an art and many leading professional clubs employ ex-keepers as coaches to

Denmark's ace goalkeeper Peter Schmeichel takes the ball off Germany's Jürgen Klinsmann in 1992's European Championship Final.

pass on their knowledge and experience. A good goalkeeper should be tall, with strong hands and shoulders. He needs to possess the agility of a gymnast, the reflexes of a tennis star, the strength and courage of a rugby forward and the ball-handling skills of a basketball player. The best keepers are also commanding and aggressive on the field with an unflappable temperament. It requires someone who can keep his emotions under control if he has made a mistake and not allow it to affect his teammates. A temperamental keeper becomes a liability when his anger and frustration unsettles the defenders in front of him.

But an extrovert keeper's antics can be positive. The Zimbabwe international goalkeeper Bruce Grobbelaar is renowned for his handstands and famous wobbly knees act to distract A.S. Roma penalty takers in the 1984 European Cup Final. Peter Schmeichel, Denmark's extrovert goalkeeper, who remains unflappable in his own box, is not averse to joining his team's attack at a corner if they are losing late in the game. Colombia's Rene Higuita often comes out of his goal to dribble the ball down the wing, or tackle an opponent outside his penalty area. He operates like a spare sweeper. But he lived too dangerously during the 1990 World Cup finals against Cameroon, when Roger Milla took the ball and went on to score.

In the modern game, goalkeepers are required to do more than just stop shots. They have an excellent view of the game and must have the vision to create moves by distributing the ball by feet, or hands to teammates in good strategic positions.

LEFT: face straight onto the ball when catching a high shot.

CENTER: cradling the ball and cushioning its impact when dealing with chest or waist-height threats.

RIGHT: in the low catch, use a raised knee to block the ball's path as you catch it.

Catching the ball at waist height

When stopping shots at waist height, the whole of the body should be behind the line of the ball, with the palms of the hands pointed upward so the ball can be scooped up and gathered safely into the chest which should be relaxed on impact to cushion the power of the shot. Wrap your hands around the ball and bend the chest forward over it. This will help to prevent the ball slipping out of your grasp.

Catching the ball at chest height

To prevent the ball bouncing off the chest when catching it, place both hands behind it when making contact. The elbows should be kept close to the body and fingers outspread.

Catching the ball above the head

Dealing with high balls and crosses is probably the most important aspect of a goalkeeper's role after stopping shots. As a keeper you have a distinct advantage over opponents because you can use your hands, and will be already on the move as the ball comes across enabling you to jump much higher.

The goalkeeper should try to take the ball at its highest point and not wait for it to drop. Get into position using short steps and carefully watching the flight of the ball. Take off with a spring, getting your arms up early and high with both hands behind the ball with fingers outspread. After catching the ball firmly with hands

Basic technique

The basic principle of goalkeeping is safety first, to get both hands on the ball, with the body behind the hands to form a second barrier. Keeping balanced is most important, but your position varies with the height, speed and direction of the ball as it comes toward you. This goes not only for your body and legs but also for your arms and hands.

Stopping a ground shot

There are two ways of stopping a shot along the ground: the stoop and the knee. For the stoop, make sure you are in direct line with the flight of the ball. Keep your legs straight and bend down at the waist. Place the hands and palms upward with the little fingers together under the ball and scoop it firmly upward into the chest, grasping it tightly with both hands.

To gather a shot in the kneeling position, move the lower half of the body and feet sideways in line with the ball. Lower one knee to the ground, level with the opposite heel, turning your chest toward the ball to form a wider barrier. Keeping your head steady and eyes on the ball, scoop the ball into the chest as before.

Way-To-Play Tips

Body behind the ball

Make sure you're fully behind the ball by moving your body and feet before getting your hands into position. Once your feet are in position, the body naturally follows.

Concentrate!

Retain concentration for the whole game. You could go for 88 minutes without having a shot to save and then, in the 89th minute, have to deal with an attacker running at you, or a dangerous high cross. Think positively all the time and don't be distracted.

Attitude

Never change your mind, or flap at the ball. Go for it positively, ignoring the other players around you.

straight at you. With clenched fists make contact with the center of the ball and send it back in the direction it came from.

When using one fist, use the arm nearest the goal-line and don't swing at the ball. The punching action should again be as straight as possible. Make sure you punch with the knuckle and aim to fist the ball as high in the air as possible. Punch the ball out at head height, or below and ball could drop to an opponent in a good scoring position.

On occasions during a game the goalkeeper may not be sure of getting two hands on the ball, so will decide to palm, or deflect it over the crossbar. Leap as if to catch the ball, but with a natural overarm swing, spread the palm and fingers to make contact and guide it over the crossbar. Be ready to stretch your arm and finger tips and dive full length if the shot is particularly powerful, or at an angle.

You should aim to reach the ball

before it drops below the level of the crossbar, but if the shot is dipping below the bar two hands might be needed. Time your jump to give an upward thrust to the hands which should be close together and bent slightly backward.

To deflect a ball around a post, follow the flight right on to the palm of your hand. Tense your wrist at the moment of impact to cushion the power of the ball and guide it around the upright.

Diving at a striker's feet

Timing is crucial to good handling, especially when diving at an attacker's feet in a one-on-one situation to smother the ball with the body. Courage is part of a goalkeeper's job, and you need a great deal of it when diving at the feet of an opponent who has broken through into the area. Injuries can occur if a keeper hesitates, or uses the wrong technique.

As you come out, get into a low

wrapped around it, clutch it to your chest, protecting it as you hit the ground. This will help you hold on to the ball if an opponent makes a challenge, or crashes into you.

Punching and deflecting the ball

There are times when a goalkeeper under pressure in a crowded penalty area or goalmouth, is forced to punch the ball away, deflect it over the crossbar, or around a post. Because of their vulnerability against tall attackers, smaller goalkeepers may prefer to punch the ball away when dealing with high crosses. A two-fisted punch is best used when the ball is coming

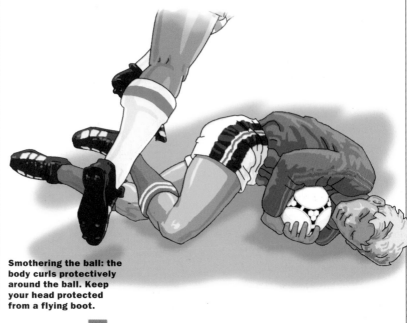

Smothering the ball: the body curls protectively around the ball. Keep your head protected from a flying boot.

Crystal Palace keeper Nigel Martyn dives to punch the ball away.

position with knees bent, head and shoulders forward and arms in front of your head. Get as low to the ground as possible when going for the ball so that your body is a yard or so behind it. Make sure your timing is right. Dive too soon and the attacker can lift the ball over your body. Dive too late and the ball could slip under your body.

Also make sure your body is along the ground at an angle before reaching for the ball. Get your body as close to the ball as you can when grabbing it from the attacker's feet and clutching it into your chest. Your head should be protected as it is behind your hands and arms and legs well away from the ball.

Kicking the ball from your hands

Like all good field players, goalkeepers should be able to use both feet and have the strength to kick the ball half the length of the field. Only being able to kick with one foot can be a great tactical disadvantage. Opponents could stand in front of you

and force you to use your weaker foot to kick out from the penalty area.

When kicking from the hand keep your eyes on the ball, and throw it well up in front of you. Be careful not to throw it too close to your body because that restricts your movements, or too far away so you have to stretch for it. Keep your head down and follow through with the kicking leg. Your body should be behind the line of the ball to avoid being off-balance and so slicing your kick.

Goal kicks

There are three types of goal kick:

The simple big boot over midfield so that your attackers can challenge for possession.

The short kick to one of your defenders to bring other teammates into play to start a move.

The chipped kick to loft the ball over opposing attackers to a teammate in space.

Accuracy is more important than brute force with goal kicking. Keep your eyes on the ball and head down. To gain more height run up at an angle and get your boot under the ball. If you want to get the ball as far downfield as possible run straight at the ball and kick through.

Throwing the ball out

When you've saved the ball, look up and see if a teammate is in a good position to start a move. If so, you might decide to throw the ball out rather than kick it. Throwing is the most accurate way of distributing the ball and keeping possession with

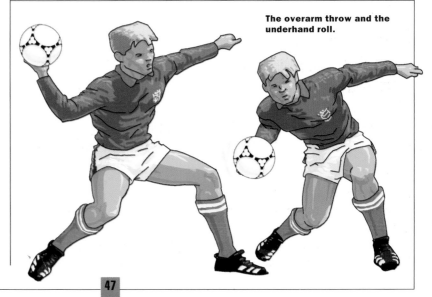

The overarm throw and the underhand roll.

Soccer Practice

Using four or five players: stand in your goal facing the strikers who are positioned around the edge of the penalty area 'D'. The strikers take it in turns to shoot at goal. After saving the shot, get back onto your feet as quickly as possible. To improve your speed, the next striker shoots at goal immediately after the previous shot is saved. Vary the exercise by trying chip shots.

In pairs: place a cone to act as a defender at an angle to the goal just inside the penalty area. Your partner runs up and dummies past the cone and shoots for goal. You come out to narrow the angle and attempt to save the shot. The attacker should vary direction around the cone and shoot with the other foot. Gradually move the cone closer to the goal.

In pairs: stand on the goal line with your back to your partner taking the kick. The kicker shouts 'ready' as contact with the ball is made. Twist to face the shot and save it. Now throw the ball back to the kicker. Repeat the exercise using different types of shot to keep you alert.

In pairs: sit on the ground three or four yards away from a partner who throws the ball toward you at varying heights and speed. As soon as it leaves your partner's hands, leap and try to save the ball.

In pairs: stand in the middle of a goal, or between two cones placed seven or eight yards apart. Your partner, 12 yards away, rolls the ball five yards to your left or right. You dive to try to save the ball. After a while, get your partner to roll the ball directly toward you. Race out from your line and dive forward to smother the ball.

In threes: to practice taking high balls, turning them over the bar or punching them away. The ball is thrown, or crossed into the goalmouth by one player, while another challenges the goalkeeper's attempts to catch the ball.

your team. Roll the ball out under-arm if your teammate is standing fairly close to you. You need to roll the ball into space just in front of him so that he can control it in his stride.

The overarm is used to throw the ball out at a greater distance. Use your non-throwing arm to point at the player you are throwing the ball to. This will help your balance. Keep your feet apart, head and body in line with the target and throwing arm straight. Bowl the ball overarm with plenty of power.

Taking steps

Remember the goalkeeper cannot take more that four steps while hold-ing, bouncing, or throwing the ball. Once the ball has been released, it cannot be touched with the keeper's hands until another player has been in contact with it. If this "four steps Law" is broken, an indirect free kick is awarded and with it the threat of a shot at goal from within the penalty area.

The back-pass rule has been dealt with on pages 16–17.

Dealing with penalty kicks

At a penalty kick the odds are heav-ily stacked in favor of the kicker. The goalkeeper is not expected to make a save. He's a hero if that happens.

Despite the odds, however, knowing how to deal with penalty kicks is becoming more important now that we have penalty shootouts decide the results of many different games.

Remember the pressure is all on the kicker, so try to gain a psycho-logical advantage by looking confi-dent as the player shapes up to take the kick. Close your mind to all the noise around you and con-centrate on the ball. As the kicker places the ball try to assess which side of the goal it's going to go. If a right-footed player uses a straight run-up the ball is more likely to be placed to your left. If a left-footed player uses a straight run-up the ball is more likely to be placed to your right. If the kicker runs at an angle, chances are it's to bend the ball with pace in the same direction as the run up. A blaster will try to hit the ball high into the net.

But whatever method the kicker is using, stay on your line and in an upright position for as long as you can. Move your body a little so you are in a position to shift your feet quickly when you have decided in which direction you are going to

Argentina's goalkeeper Luis Islas takes the ball off Nigeria's Rashidi Yakini to break up this attack during the 1994 World Cup.

throw yourself. But don't be too disappointed if you fail to make a save.

Learning the angles

Good positioning is a vital part of a goalkeeper's game and one of the most difficult to learn. Shots are easier to save with good positioning. Goals are easily scored if a goalkeeper stands rooted to a spot on the goal line. The aim is to make the goalkeeper appear as a large obstacle to an attacker and insure challengers see as little of the goal as possible.

The goalkeeper must come off the line and move toward the attacker, narrowing the angle of the target area. Timing is important. Come out too far and the attacker could lob the ball over your head. Come out too soon and the attacker could dribble the ball around you, or slide it under your falling body.

It's also important to remain on your feet with arms outstretched, presenting as large a barrier as possible to block the attacker's route to goal.

If the attacker runs in from the flank, you should move across to narrow the angle and be positioned on the far side of the goal so you have the space in which to stop a cross.

The Wales goalkeeper Neville Southall is brilliant at getting himself in the correct position for any situation. He often makes great saves look easy because he has positioned himself in exactly the right spot to take the ball cleanly. Spectacular goalkeepers are rarely the best goalkeepers.

During corner kicks you should position yourself at the post furthest away from the ball. You will then be able to move forward when the ball is kicked.

Way-To-Play Tips

Punching clear
Young goalkeepers should always punch the ball in the direction they are facing. Experienced keepers with strong hands and arms can use the back of the hand to knock the ball to safety.

Warm-up
Before a game it's important for goalkeepers to warm-up with gentle stretching exercises. Then get team-mates to launch balls at you from all angles, heights and distances.

Weights
Weight training under supervision will help strengthen your arms, shoulders, wrists and thighs. All are essential parts of the body for a keeper.

Communication
As goalkeeper you are in command of the penalty area. Make sure your defenders are aware of attackers moving into space, or making blind-side runs, and shout loudly when you are going for crosses. This way you can avoid any confusion.

Attack! Attack!
Keepers don't just defend, you can look to set up an attack by distributing the ball quickly, either by kicking, or throwing it out. A long kick upfield can catch opposing defenses out, and a quick throw to a winger or midfielder can start an attacking move before they have a chance to reorganize.

Tactics

YOUNGSTERS should concentrate on learning the basic soccer skills and simply enjoy playing before trying to understand the different systems and tactics that are now very much part of the modern game.

But as you progress it is essential to have an understanding of the formations and patterns of play. Soccer is a team game and the manager, or coach, should decide on a system that makes the best use of the players available to him. A good playing system uses players' strengths to the full and covers up their weaknesses.

But systems alone do not win games. It is the players working within the team formation who get the results. So, it's important that the manager, or coach, explains the system to all the players in the squad to ensure they are familiar and happy with their roles.

No system, nor tactics, should ignore the individual talents of the team's more skilled players. Everyone likes to see players performing their magic in games, but those skills should be used for the benefit of the whole team.

Basically, tactics are plans from which teams work to get the ball into the opposing danger area to score goals and to stop their opponents from doing the same.

Before the great Hungarians defeated England 6–3 at Wembley in 1953 with a new style of play, the then-prevalent English game was based on 2–3–5 formation: a goalkeeper, two fullbacks, a center-half, two halfbacks and five forwards (two wingers, two inside-forwards and a center-forward).

The Hungarians played with a center-forward deep in midfield and with two attacking inside-forwards. The England center-half was pulled out of position, while the two fullbacks stayed deep which gave the Hungarian inside-forwards Sandor Kocsis and Ferenc Puskas space in which to cause havoc.

The result shocked world football and within a few years the Hungarian style of play had completely revolutionized the game. Instead of kick-and-rush, or push-and-run, tactics and systems evolved which enabled teams to make better use of their players and to compete and be successful at the highest level.

The Brazilian World Cup-winning team in 1958 used four defenders across the back to deny the opposing wingers space. From this start, teams began to play with four players forward and two in midfield. So the 4–2–4 and then 4–3–3 systems were born.

Throughout the 1960s and 1970s the game became more defensive with fewer attackers and more players in midfield. Tactics were amended and devised accordingly.

England won the World Cup in 1966 without the use of wingers and the rest of football followed England manager Alf Ramsey's plan. In the place of wingers came midfielders who controlled the game. These days World Cups have been won with teams using five players in midfield with just one attacker, as Argentina did in 1986.

In England at club level, Liverpool has on occasions used a sweeper with three defenders at the back, five in midfield and one man at the front as the lone striker. The reason for this defensive formation is simple: flooding the midfield makes it difficult for opponents to mark the midfielders.

Modern systems work successfully because players are more flexible, with midfield players and strikers often being required to move back to help out in defense, while defenders often support the attack with runs down the flanks.

Soccer is an easy game to play, but tactics and systems are becoming more and more sophisticated as managers, or coaches continually work out plans to outwit their opponents.

So a study of team tactics and formations will help to improve your skills and provide a better understanding of the modern game and how it should be played at all levels.

OPPOSITE: Franco Baresi, of A.C. Milan and Italy, is one of the world's top defenders.

① TEAM FORMATIONS

A team positions its players in any one of the 17 positions shown in Diagram A. The choice of formation depends on the system chosen by the coach. All systems should be flexible to take into account weather conditions, the opposition, the competition, field and players.

On cold, hard, icy surfaces smaller players can keep their footing better than taller because of the lower center of gravity; in wet, muddy conditions strength is required; and players not fully fit could struggle on a hot, humid afternoon.

Think positively. There is no use playing 4–4–2 if the opposition is playing that way unless your aim is to cancel each other out. Good coaches will have done their homework and should use tactics to counter their opponents. They will also have worked out the strengths and weaknesses of the opposition. If the opposing winger is their danger person the coach won't want to have a young, inexperienced fullback doing the marking.

If a team is playing in a Cup competition over two

Diagram A

1. Goalkeeper	10. Right midfield
2. Sweeper	11. Center midfield
3. Right back	12. Left midfield
4. Right centerback	13. Right winger
5. Left centerback	14. Right striker
6. Left back	15. Center striker
7. Right half/wing back	16. Left striker
8. Central defender	17. Left winger
9. Left half/wing back	

games, a tie might be good enough. So, the coach may decide on a defensive formation, especially if the game is away from home. Teams generally prefer to play attacking tactics at home, on familiar ground. If one or two star players are injured, the coach may decide to change the tactics slightly to suit the players who are available.

4–2–4

Different nations tend to play different techniques. For example, 30 years ago most English clubs used a 4–2–4 or 4–3–3 system. The benefit of 4–2–4 (Diagram B) is that you can have six players attacking, or defending. When defending, two midfield players pull back to help the defense. When attacking they can move forward to support their strikers. You would also be looking for the two fullbacks to break forward in support. The success of this formation depends on the ability and stamina of the midfielders to continually link with attack and defense. This is a good system to adopt if your team has two fast wingers and the players able to distribute long, accurate passes to the strikers.

Diagram B

4–3–3

This system (Diagram C) gives you strength through the midfield having three players in this area. You also have the option of using seven defensive players and six in attack, depending on which team has the ball. When your team has the ball, the three midfield players can make late forward runs adding more power to the attack. Use this system if your team likes to build attacks with passes.

4–4–2

A defensive formation (Diagram D), is often used when a team has a shortage of strikers, or a surplus of midfielders. This allows you to get eight players back behind the ball when you are defending. When you are attacking there are four players available to support the strikers with the two wide midfield players used as wingers. Great pressure is put on the two strikers who must be capable of holding the ball when under pressure until their midfielders can support them.

5–3–2

The sweeper system (Diagram E) is a defensive formation used for absorbing relentless pressure and launching quick counter-attacks. Although primarily defensive, used correctly it can become an effective attacking formation. When the opportunity arises, the two fullbacks push forward to support the three midfielders. Many European teams such as Barcelona of Spain use this system with slight variations.

4–5–1

An ultra-defensive system (Diagram F) which is very difficult for teams to break down. When attacking, the ball has to be passed accurately and the midfield players have to break forward to support the striker. At international level, France won the European Championship in 1984 under Michel Platini's captaincy, with five in midfield and a lone striker up front.

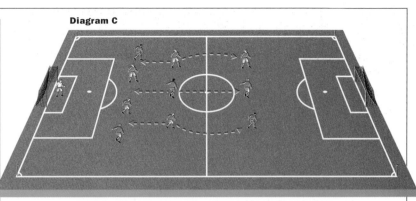
Diagram C

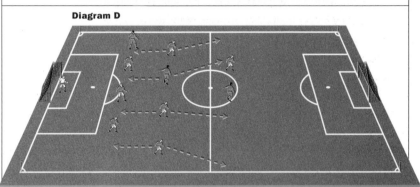
Diagram D

Diagram E

Diagram F

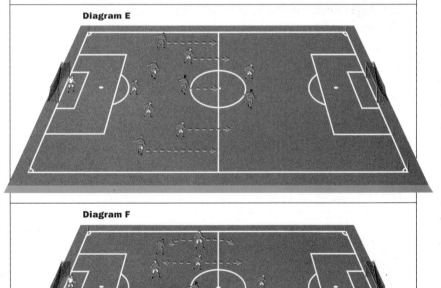

Goalkeepers

Diagram A

The prime function of the goalkeeper is to stop goals being scored against their team. However, they are more than the last line of defense, they can be the springboards for attack. The keeper should start an attacking movement by throwing the ball to a nearby teammate. He could also use a long kick upfield to catch the opposition out. Goalkeepers should take command of the penalty area and keep talking to the defense. If the team is under pressure, the goal-keeper can slow the game down to allow the defense to regroup before releasing the ball. But don't get a yellow card for time-wasting.

Because of their position, goal-keepers have a panoramic view of the whole Field Of Play and can spot problems building up for defenders. They can also see attacking opportunities when spaces occur, or team-mates are left unmarked. The goal-keeper can also act as a sweeper, moving out of the penalty area with the ball to pass to a defender, or midfielder in space.

Remember, the keeper's positional skills are also vital at all corner kicks, dead-ball situations—especially when organizing a defensive wall—and when the opposition is attacking.

A goalkeeper must also be ready for the unexpected, such as a rebound, sliced kick, mistimed pass by a defender, or a snap shot from an opposing striker.

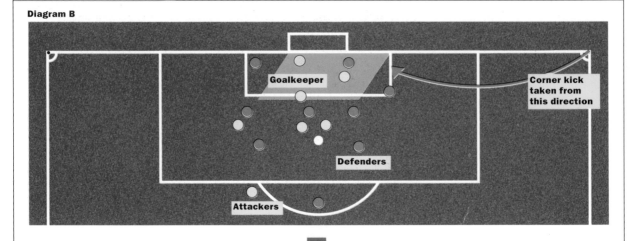

Diagram B

Goalkeeper

Corner kick taken from this direction

Defenders

Attackers

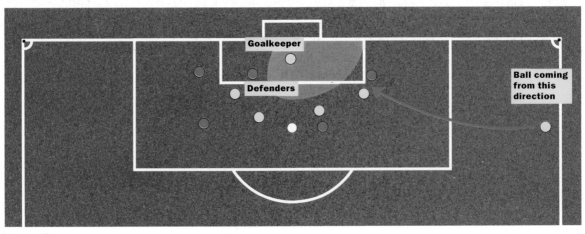

Diagram C

Diagram A shows where a goalkeeper should be positioned to narrow the angle and reduce the target area a striker has to aim at.

A goalkeeper is expected to gather all high balls in the goal area. Diagram B shows where the keeper should be positioned for a corner kick taken from the right. If you're playing as the keeper, you should be in the ideal position to cover the shaded area. Your defenders can adjust their positions to counter the danger when the ball is crossed.

For a fierce drive, or cross to the near post, you should be positioned a yard or so off the goal line (as in Diagram C) from where you can see the danger and follow the flight of the ball more easily. Notice how the defenders have moved to cover the shaded danger zone behind the keeper. One defender has even moved to stand on the goal line.

A goalkeeper is responsible for organizing the defense for free kicks around the penalty area. This must be done quickly. In Diagram D, a free kick has been awarded about 25 yards from goal. The goalkeeper has positioned a wall of four defenders ten yards from the ball, with defender (A) standing slightly outside a line between the ball and the near post. If the keeper's line of vision is reduced, it may be better to take defender (B) out of the wall. The goalkeeper now has a large area of goal covered and can move forward, or along the goal line to save the ball if it gets past the wall.

Diagram D

Fullbacks, Sweepers and Centerbacks

The fullback's task is to mark, cover and tackle. Essentially, playing this position, you have to stop attacking moves by closing down the opposing winger and force the attack to go inside to prevent the ball being crossed into the goal area. You should also cover your centerback, protect the goalkeeper, clear the keeper's lines when under pressure, support the midfield and link up with the wingers. Modern fullbacks also attack down the flanks and get crosses in at every opportunity.

Italy's Paolo Maldini has all the necessary qualities to be a top-class fullback, and in the 1994 World Cup showed himself to be the world's best. Two excellent attacking fullbacks are Jorginho and Leonardo, both of Brazil.

You also need to have the pace to match the winger you're marking. If you have no wide player to cover, you should support your defensive partners and look out for opposing players making late runs so that you can block their path to goal.

Sweepers

The "Sweeper" (Diagram A), or "Libero" as this role is called in Europe, does not have to mark anyone in particular. When playing this roving role behind the back three or four, you should be ready to intercept attackers who have made late runs past the central defenders. As a sweeper, you should be ready to collect or "sweep-up" any loose balls. You should also be a good tackler, header of the ball, passer and reader of the game. From the sweeper's position behind the back four you should be able to spot attacking moves building up. The sweeper can also perform a vital attacking role. Generally you are unmarked and know exactly where teammates are positioned.

The former Bayern Munich and West Germany star, Franz Beckenbauer, was a very successful attacking sweeper during the 1970s. As a former midfield player, "Der Kaiser" (as he was nicknamed) was able to collect the ball deep in his own half and then set off on a run, or start an attacking move with a long, accurately flighted pass.

Excellent distribution is a vital factor and one of the best examples of the last decade is Holland's Ronald Koeman.

Centerbacks

Most teams have two centerbacks who are the kingpins of defense. In this position you're covering the area where attackers most want to be and so you are under almost as much pressure as the goalkeeper. Any mistake you make could lead to a goal. You must develop a firm understanding with your partner centerback. It is important that each of you knows when the other

Nigeria's Daniel Amokachi can't get around Italy's brilliant defender Paolo Maldini during their World Cup '94 match.

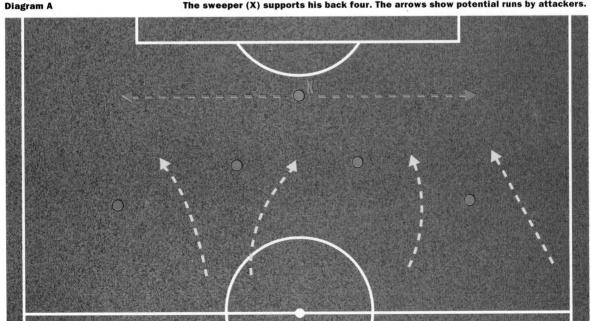

Two attackers (reds) are about to put pressure on the centerbacks and work an opening. The left back reduces the threat by moving across and covering his central defenders.

is about to make a challenge, so either can provide support. The taller of the two normally takes the more central position because of the obvious advantage in the air dealing with crosses and defensive headers. The other centerback will play diagonally behind, ready to deal with movements along the ground.

Power in the air is essential for centerbacks. You must completely dominate the strikers you're marking, especially in the penalty area. Often this means giving away a corner, instead of heading the ball out into space where an alert opponent can seize on the clearance and shoot for goal, or maintain the pressure by crossing back in the danger zone. Centerbacks must have the pace to move forward in attack and

to recover if they get caught out of position, or mistime a tackle. If you are the taller player you will often support attacks at corner kicks, where your aerial power can do a great deal of damage. Players in this position often make ideal captains. Franco Baresi of Italy and Bobby Moore of England's 1966 World Cup-winning team are both excellent examples.

Diagram A   **The sweeper (X) supports his back four. The arrows show potential runs by attackers.**

Midfielders

The midfield is where most games are won or lost. Take command of the midfield and you'll dominate the game. So, good midfielders are essential to all teams. They are soccer's utility men.

Essentially, they must possess the vision to read a game, have good ball control, pace, the ability to tackle, mark and distribute the ball over short and long distances. Midfielders are the play-makers, the brains, the engine room that drives a team, the vital link between defense and attack. They break up attacks by the opposing team, start attacks for their own side, close in for the kill and even shoot at goal if the opportunity presents itself.

Because midfielders do more running than any other player on the field, they need excellent fitness and stamina. Top class midfielders to watch are players such as Enzo Scifo of Belgium, Italy's Dino Baggio, Krassimir Balakov of Bulgaria, Demetrio Albertini of Milan and Italy, Germany's Thomas Doll, Holland's Wim Jonk, the U.S.A.'s John Harkes

Germany's Lothar Matthäus is tackled by Brazil's Dunga. Both these great midfielders are equally comfortable in defense.

and England's Paul Gascoigne.

A strong tackling midfield player can usually operate in a more defensive role by winning the ball and containing the opposition in the central area before driving his team forward—rather like former England and Manchester United captain Bryan Robson.

Skilled ball-playing midfielders are better equipped to break forward quickly with the ball to start an attack, or hold the ball until a teammate can move into position.

Midfielders must be prepared to do a great deal of unselfish running with-

Diagram A

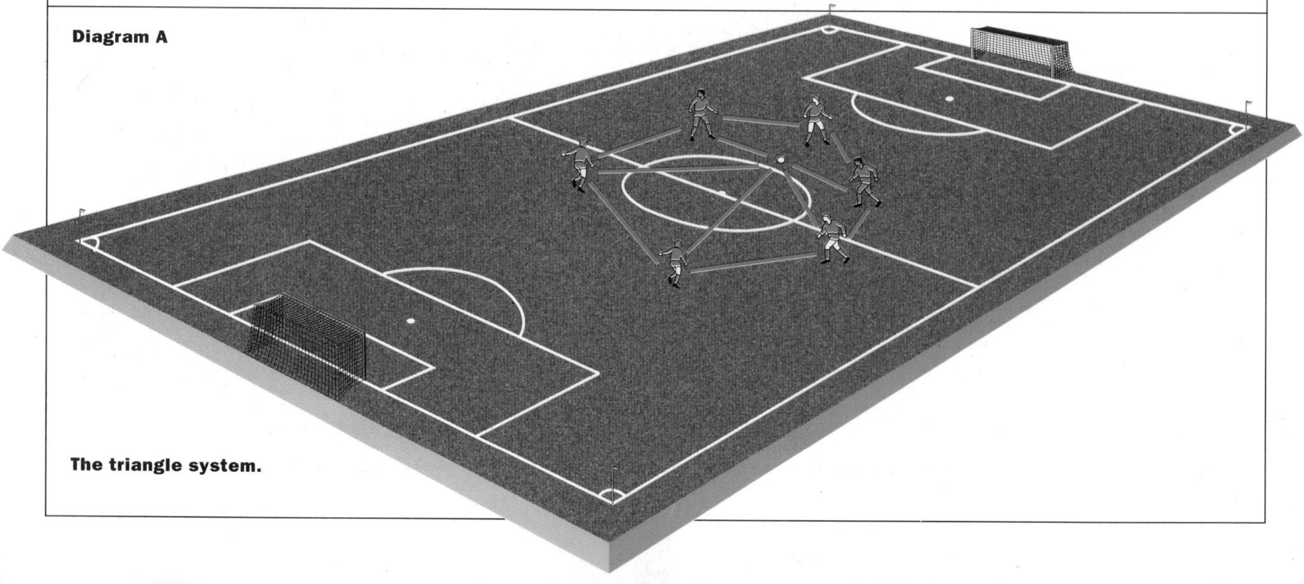

The triangle system.

Diagram B

Attackers (A) and (B) are
being marked by two
defenders. Midfielder (C)
runs into space to support
(A) and (B).

out the ball to support teammates in the last two-thirds of the filed. Clever running off the ball creates space, gives teammates various options and catches opposing defenders off guard. They might be distracted by your movement long enough to allow a teammate to dribble past, move into the extra space provided or make a defense-splitting pass.

An attacking midfielder in possession of the ball often has to decide whether to hold on to it allowing teammates time to move into posi-

tion, or to deliver a short, or long pass. Passing the ball is obviously the quicker of the two options.

Long passes delivered from midfield behind defenders can launch quick attacks, bending the ball with the inside or outside of the foot around them. If you're playing against a team with a sweeper, passes out to the wings are much more effective than dribbling through the packed defense.

Most midfield play operates on the "triangle" system that allows each

player at least two options of where to pass the ball (see Diagram A).

Supporting the front-runners is an essential part of midfield play. In Diagram B the midfielder runs into space to support the two attackers who are being closely marked by defenders, giving them another option.

A long accurate pass through a crowded midfield area (see Diagram C) can often create a scoring opportunity if players are quick to spot the move and run off the ball.

Diagram C

Midfielder (A) delivers a pass to (B). The defenders are pulled out of position by attackers (C, D, E) and (F) running off the ball.

Strikers and Wingers

Goals win matches—so it's not surprising that top goalscorers are the most wanted and valued men in soccer. Today's ace strikers, like Manchester United's $11 million-man Andy Cole, England star Alan Shearer, Holland's Marco van Basten and Germany's Jürgen Klinsmann, are worth their weight in goals because they have the natural ability to put the ball in the back of the net. They have an insatiable hunger for goals.

As a modern-day striker, like Brazil's brilliant Romario, you need to have pace to lose a marker, strength to hold off challenges, ball control to retain possession and beat an opponent. You must also have the courage to take the knocks that occur when tightly marked, and the confidence to keep shooting even when the going gets tough.

But good forward play by a striker concerns more than just scoring goals. You should be able to set up chances for teammates, by acting as a target man, or a decoy, to draw defenders away from the middle of the field and create space for them to exploit.

In this role, you often receive the ball facing your own goal and should be comfortable when balls are knocked in to you from all areas of the field. Be like Welsh international, Mark Hughes. His strength and determination enable him to knock the ball down into the path of a teammate who is running into the penalty area, or six-yard box to shoot for goal. Sweden's Martin Dahlin is another good example.

As the target man you must make yourself available throughout the whole game, and be prepared to have a constant battle with defenders as you wait for crosses and passes from teammates.

But whether you have the mobility of Jürgen Klinsmann or the strength of Mark Hughes, you should always be concentrating, trying to anticipate the unexpected and be ready to seize a half-chance in front of goal.

Good strikers do not wait for chances to open up; they are continually on the move looking to play their part in attacking moves. In Diagram A, the striker A has collected the ball on the halfway line, passes to B who passes to C, who crosses for him to score after making a well-timed run.

Wingers

Wingers are usually attacking midfielders, who play wide on the flanks. The old-fashioned wingers would wait for the ball to be passed to them. Recent equivalents, such as Marc Overmars of Holland and Russia's Andre Kanchelskis, are expected to attack, defend and go looking for the ball if necessary.

Diagram A

Striker (A) starts and finishes a goal-scoring move. He passes to (B), who passes to (C), who crosses for (A2) to score.

England international Ian Wright in spectacular action during Arsenal's 1993–94 European Cup-winners' Cup tie against Paris St. Germain.

vision to know when to hold the ball up (retain possession) until support arrives, when to cross early and when to cut inside to attack the target. There is no use a winger making a dazzling run down the flank and crossing the ball if there's nobody available. Equally there is no point in running inside to the penalty area if it is crowded with players.

When a fullback makes a break down the flank, the winger should be prepared to drop back and cover that position if possession is lost. Wingers and fullbacks generally work together to create an overlap. This involves a winger in possession passing to an unmarked teammate on the flank. He then runs around his marker to either receive a return pass in stride from the overlapper or act as a decoy, leaving the marker stranded. The problem with the overlap is that if an attacking player loses possession they are both left out of position (Diagram B).

Wingers create space on the flanks, run at fullbacks and cross the ball to their central attackers from the sideline, or move inside to shoot for goal. Crosses made from the goal line must curve away from the goal. If a defender is running back with an attacker he will find it hard to clear the ball without conceding a corner or throw-in near his line, while the goalkeeper may struggle to reach the cross.

Obviously wide players need pace. They must also have the

Diagram B

Defender (A) passes the ball to his winger, (B). Defender (A) then runs around his marker to take a return pass from (B).

Switching the point of attack

Defenders are vulnerable when they are pulled out of position by opponents who suddenly switch the point of attack and get the ball into space where there is no cover.

They are also handicapped when forced to turn by an attacker who gets in behind them. A "switch movement" by an attacker can often unbalance a defender because he is forced to turn around in order to keep the game in full view. Teams will switch the direction of play by building an attack on one side of the field, say the left. So the defense shapes to cover the left side, anticipating a break-through. In doing so, if the defense leaves a gap on the

right side, an attacker should run into the space ready to take a pass from the left.

The player with the ball should then switch the point of attack with a pass across the pitch to his teammate who has just run into the open space. This movement forces the opposing defense to regroup to deal with the new situation, costing them the advantage.

But forwards are not the only players who can switch the direction of play to build an attack. The goalkeeper should be looking to throw the ball out to the wings at every opportunity. A fullback pushing forwards might get in two or three

passes on his side of the field and then switch play with a 30-yard pass to a teammate on the opposite flank. Suddenly switching play in this situation also gives the defense a chance to get back into position before losing possession.

This tactic can be particularly effective when making a direct attack on goal. In Diagram A the central striker (A) begins to move toward the right flank and teammate (C), but suddenly turns and passes to his left winger (B) who has run into space created by defender (Y) moving across to cover his central defender (Z) against the possible threat developing down the middle.

Diagram A

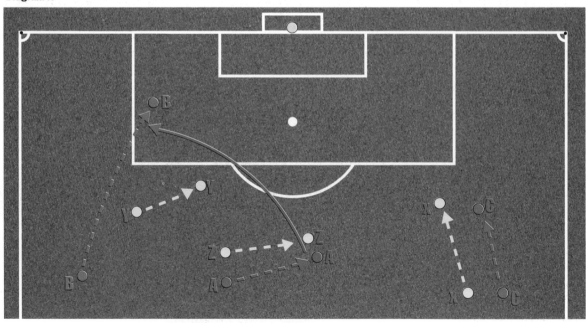

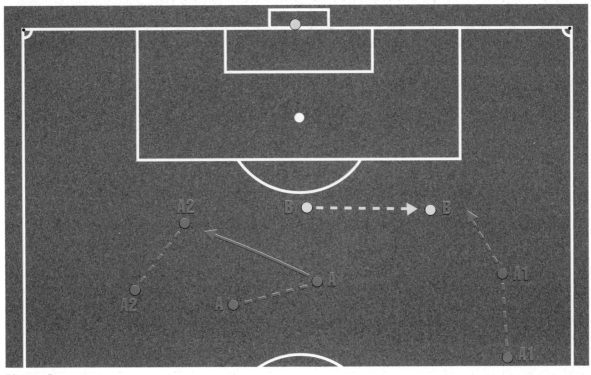

Diagram B

Switching the direction of attack requires good vision and an awareness of the pattern of play being used by the opposition. Pace, accuracy, anticipation and determination are obviously important. So is feinting to deceive opponents.

Italian defender, Paolo Maldini, is one of the finest examples of a player with the ability to turn defense into attack with a long pass or penetrating run.

In Diagram B, attacker (A) shapes to pass the ball to (A1). Defender (B) moves across to cover, but (A) switches play and passes to (A2).

In Diagram C midfielder (A) has possession and two teammates (B) and (C) move into position to receive a pass. Midfielder (A) suddenly turns toward teammate (B) on his right. At the same time a second midfielder (D) runs through the gap created by attacker (C) moving out left and takes a pass from midfielder (A) leaving him with a clear run on goal.

Diagram C

In this example attackers (B) and (C) make decoy runs allowing (D) to make an unchallenged run into the penalty area. An accurate pass from (A) leaves (D) with a good scoring opportunity.

④ COUNTER-ATTACKING

ATTACKS can start as soon as the ball is won. Counter-attacking begins when the defending team waits for the opposition to attack, then wins the ball in its half of the field and gets it forward as quickly as possible.

Attacking teams must always be aware that they can be caught out with a quick counter-attack if they lose possession after getting too many players forward.

Speed is the essential element of successful counter-attacking once the ball has been won. At least one player should be positioned wide to receive a pass and hold the ball to give supporting players the opportunity to make their runs into the opposing penalty area to meet a cross, or a returned pass.

Diagram A

Defender (A) gains possession, passes to (B) who runs forward. (A) runs inside and receives the ball from (B) to shoot.

Diagram B

Defender (A) wins the ball in his own half and lofts an accurate 30-yard pass to (B) who is in a good position to run for goal.

Support Play

Good counter-attacking also depends on other members of the team playing a supporting role by pushing up to get opponents out of their half. They should also be ready to pounce on loose balls from hasty clearances or rebounds.

Defenders often make good counter-attacking players after gaining possession. In Diagram A right back (A) has won the ball and quickly passes to his winger (B) and shouts "Hold it (and the player's name)!" Right back (A) then runs wide and behind his winger. When level with the winger he calls for the ball back and runs toward the opposition penalty area to either shoot for goal, or cross to teammate (C) who has made a good forward run.

In Diagram B defender (A) has gained possession to break up an attack. He spots striker (B) in an onside position inside the opposition half and delivers a 30-yard pass to set striker (C) off on a run at goal.

Playing in the "hole"

This is a term to describe a player who plays, or pushes up into an area just behind the two main strikers (see Diagram C). The player in the "hole" could be a midfielder, a winger or even another striker taking up that supporting position.

Playing in the "hole" can prove to be an effective attacking tactic because it gives the opposition's midfield and defense a problem as to who should be marking the extra player.

It is important to inspire in all of your attacking players the confi-dence and ability to take on defenders in one-on-one situations. In modern football, defenses are so well organized that it is often the dribbling skills which can make all the difference between success or failure when sides are evenly matched.

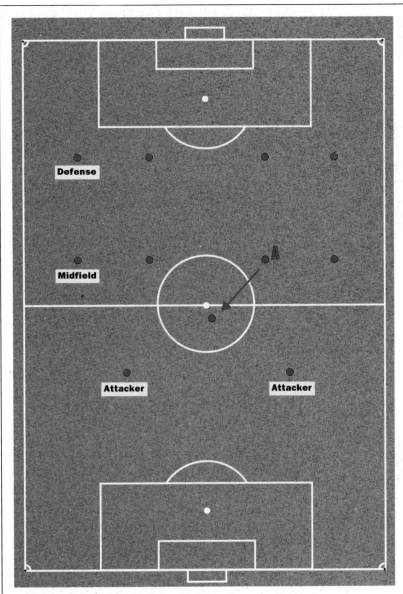

Diagram C
Player (A) moves forward into the "hole" behind the two attackers.

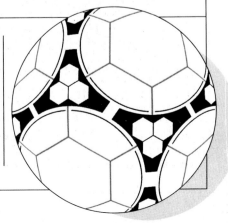

THE long-ball game has been given something of a bad reputation by soccer purists. They claim this direct style of getting the ball forward to the strikers as quickly as possible requires little skill and reduces midfield play.

This is unfair to what can be a very effective style of attacking play. When performed correctly, the long-ball game demands a very high level of skill from not only the passer of the ball, but from the attacker receiving it.

The player making a long pass should insure the ball lands behind a defender. If the opposition is playing with a sweeper the ball should be lofted out more to the wings. Against a tight defense, a long-ball pass down the center to a teammate who has made an angled run can often

catch the opposition out and result in a goal being scored.

In October 1993, Sampdoria's Roberto Mancini hit a 45-yard pass to Ruud Gullit, enabling the Dutch master to strike a thunderous 30-yard shot past the Milan goalkeeper to give his team a 3–2 victory over the Italian champions. Nobody considered Sampdoria a boring and unimaginative team!

The long-ball down the middle, is an excellent way of beating the offside trap when the defense is well-organized, because the runner can come from deep to chase the ball. Very few defenses have the confidence to stick to their tactics when their line is breached by a player running from inside his own half a couple of times.

Who does what?

There are two elements to the long pass: the passer's accuracy in finding a teammate at long range, and the skill of the receiver to control the ball and then create, or take the chance that comes from the pass.

In the late 1970s and early-1980s, France's Michel Platini was one of the world's greatest players because of his superb all-around soccer talent. He was probably the best passer of a ball ever to play for France. But no one remembers quick one-twos with Alain Giresse, Jean Tigana, Didier Six or Dominique Rocheteau; what the fans remember is when Platini sprayed passes all over the field,

more often than not finding teammates in good positions.

Platini's passing skills would have been wasted if he didn't have players around him who could do the

The four diagrams here show the long ball that led to France's goal against England in the first round of the 1982 World Cup in Spain. France is in white shirts and blue shorts, attacking from the right. England is in red, white and blue.

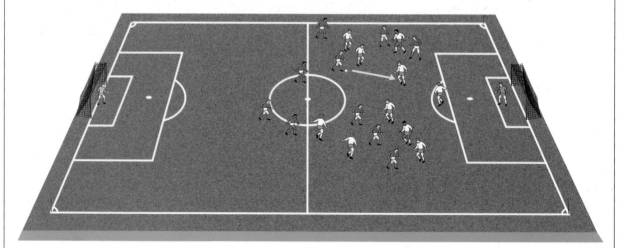

An England attack breaks down deep in France's half of the field. The French now launch a counter-strike of devastating simplicity.

Michel Platini intercepts the ball and plays a 10-yard pass to fellow midfielder Alain Giresse. The England team, however, seems to have plenty of cover.

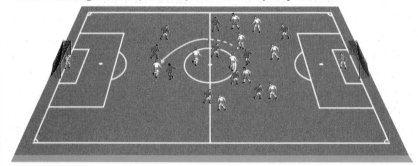

Giresse takes a few steps with the ball and then hits a beautifully weighted, right-foot pass to split the England defense. Danger looms.

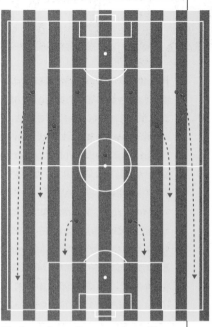

Diagram shows the correct positioning for playing in the channels.

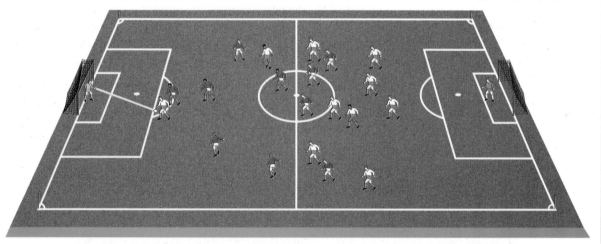

The ball lands perfectly in the path of Gérard Soler, who has made a well-timed run. He deftly controls the ball, and guides a shot past Peter Shilton into the England goal.

simple things: trapping the ball, heading, turning past a defender, timing a run. With these skills, France took the soccer world by storm, and very nearly reached the 1982 World Cup Final.

The long-ball game, if used as a part of your tactical gameplan, can be skilful and prove a very effective surprise weapon—as the diagrams on these two pages show.

Playing the channels

Defenders can set up moves in their own half of the pitch by delivering the ball into an imaginary channel in the opposition's half (see the diagram top right). Strikers can make their moves knowing the ball will be passed into these areas. The channels are wide areas of the field, so unless the ball is hit with too much power it will not run through to the goalkeeper. If the ball is played with quality into a channel and does not run out of play, it can put the opposition under a great deal of pressure.

6 SET-PIECE PLAY

A fact not often appreciated in the height of battle is that during a game the ball is out of play almost as often as it is in play. This leads to the equally surprising fact that many goals are scored just after the ball has gone dead—these goals come from set-pieces. Also remember that, unless the dead-ball kick is a penalty, the kicker is under less pressure. More pressure is on the defenders.

Teams must plan and practice taking dead ball kicks so that players are aware of what is expected of them. Coaches should work on different routines to avoid being too predictable. They shouldn't just concentrate on the players taking the kicks, either. The players not involved in taking free kicks have an important job to do. Their roles include making decoy runs and moving into various positions to distract and stretch the opposition. Free kicks, direct or indirect, can occur anywhere on the field and require more adaptability and imagination.

Set-plays should be kept relatively simple. If too many players are involved confusion often results in the kick being wasted.

Just have two, or at most three players line up to take a free kick. The opposition will be kept guessing as to which player is going to take the kick, and whether it's going to be a shot, side-foot pass or floated cross.

Quick free kicks

When you are taking a free kick or corner kick, it's best to cross the ball with plenty of pace. This is far harder to defend against than letting the ball "hang" in the air, and restricts the possibility of the defense correcting a lack of concentration in its marking.

Providing the referee lets you, and your players are where the situation calls for them to be, quickly taken free kicks keep the game flowing and don't allow the opposition much time to organize a defense. They also guarantee possession being retained—so often a free kick is squandered unneccessarily.

Throw-ins

A throw-in taken deep in the opposition's half of the field can be an effective attacking weapon. It should always be regarded as an opportunity to make a through pass and not merely a means of restarting play. The player taking the throw is often

For a right-side corner, Ipswich have a left-footed player taking this near-post, inswinging kick against Arsenal.

left unmarked and is therefore in the ideal position to receive the ball back. In this situation, throw the ball to the feet of the receiving teammate, who can more easily control and return it.

When a teammate has moved away from a marker, aim to throw the ball alongside the player so that it can be taken on the stride.

Use a long-throw player when the ball goes out of play near the opposition's penalty area. The long reach is an opportunity to get the ball to the opposition goal's near post.

Corners

This excellent attacking opportunity can be played to wherever you feel you have the best chance to take advantage of the situation. Inform your teammates of the intended target when taking a corner kick. This information can be relayed by previously agreed hand signals (like calls in baseball and football, these should be kept secret). Keep the signals simple, though. One raised arm might mean an inswinger, for instance, two raised arms an outswinger.

Near-post corner

The target is the corner of the goal area and the near post for an

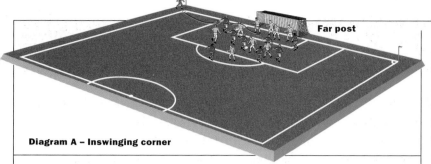

Diagram A – Inswinging corner

Far post

attacker to run in and flick the ball on at an angle, or deflect in backward. This inswinging corner (see Diagram A) is particularly difficult to defend against because it provides the attacking team with options to alter the attack.

Far-post corner

The basic corner kick aimed at the far side of the penalty area and far post, is easier to defend against than the near-post variation (see Diagram B).

The cross has to be accurate over a longer distance. Defenders have more time to deal with the threat and goalkeepers see more of the ball, making it far easier to attack and collect.

It is important to position players at the near post to block the goalkeeper's view and keep defenders guessing. The kicker should curl the ball into the penalty area for a tall attacker to take the height advantage and head at goal, or knock the ball down to cause confusion, or into a teammate's path to get a shot in.

The short corner

If the kicker spots an unmarked teammate close in, there's an option to play a short pass. The receiving player can either take the ball along the goal line before crossing, pull it back outside the penalty area for a

long shot at goal, or play it back to the corner kicker who has run wide.

Short corners can force defenders out of the penalty area, leaving gaps behind them for the attacking team to exploit.

Attacking free kicks

Any free kick awarded up to 25 yards from goal is a potential scoring opportunity for the attacking team, as defenders have to be ten yards from the ball. A free kick within shooting distance also forces the opposition to set up a defensive wall.

You can cause this defensive wall serious problems by bending the ball around it, but it's a move requiring great skill. England defender Stuart Pearce scored from a brilliant curling free kick for Nottingham Forest against Tottenham Hotspur in England's 1990–91 FA Cup Final. Another option is to side-foot the ball into the path of a teammate for him to shoot at goal.

When free kicks are taken, placing attackers in the opposition's

wall can screen the goalkeeper and upset the defenders—they concentrate on the interloper rather than the kicker. An attacker in the wall can also move just as the kick is taken, making a hole for the kicker to aim at. If the shot goes through the wall, the goalkeeper may not see the ball until the last moment. Also have one or two players making dummy runs into the penalty area to confuse the opposition further.

Penalty kicks

Taking penalty kicks is all about confidence. If you are not happy about taking a penalty, don't! Placing the penalty kick needs great accuracy. Choose the spot you are aiming at and go for it—don't change your mind during the run-up. Aiming at the corner of the back of the net makes it virtually impossible for the goalkeeper to reach the ball. A little sway, or feint of the body as you run up makes it more difficult for the goalkeeper to decide which side you are aiming at.

Blasting a penalty kick relies on power and accuracy. With the longer run-up necessary, more care is needed in deciding where to put the ball. Once the run's started, stick to your decision and keep your eyes on the ball, not the goalkeeper. Get your body over the ball and strike low, following through with the kicking leg.

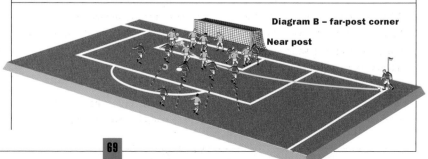

Diagram B – far-post corner

Near post

⑦ COVERING AND MARKING

ALL SUCCESSFUL teams are built on well-organized, strong defense. The main task of any defense is to stop the opposition scoring by marking attackers closely and denying them the space in which to move with the ball.

Good defending is also all about winning the ball back as quickly as possible and launching counter-attacks.

In the past, defense mainly consisted of a goalkeeper, two full backs who marked two wingers and a big, tall center half who controlled the central area in front of the goal.

In the modern game, defenders have to be as fast, athletic and as skilled as the forwards they are marking. To defend well, you must also have good tactical awareness in order to adjust to the various conditions and strategies of the opposition.

Good defending also relies on teamwork and developing an almost telepathic understanding with your fellow defenders. You must know each other's capabilities and shortcomings; you must also be aware of your teammates' positions during a game.

Communication is another vital requirement. Defenders must talk to each other constantly. Don't be afraid to shout instructions to teammates, to warn them of challenges, tell them where and when to pass the ball. A good call in the penalty area, for example at a corner, can often prevent two defenders going for the same ball and getting in each other's way.

It is essential that defenders learn and master the art of positioning. Always insure you are between your opponent and the ball. Restrict an opponent's space by jockeying him into positions where he can't be a threat, and don't allow him to get so close so that he can easily turn you.

World-class defenders such as Italy's Paolo Maldini don't commit themselves in a challenge for the ball unless they are sure of winning it (or that a teammate is covering for them). If you fail to win the ball in a tackle, your opponent will have your teammate to contend with and not be given a clear run.

Diagram A

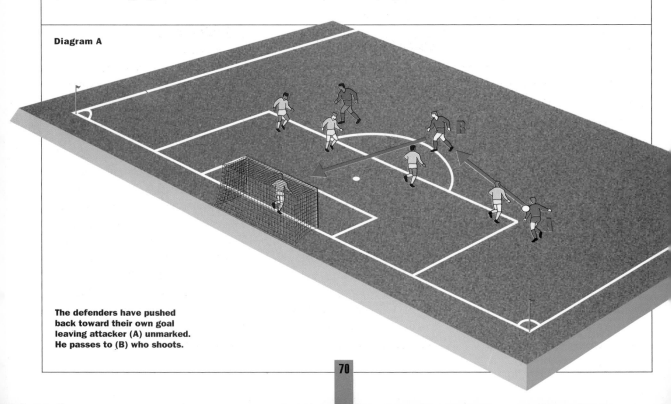

The defenders have pushed back toward their own goal leaving attacker (A) unmarked. He passes to (B) who shoots.

Diagram B

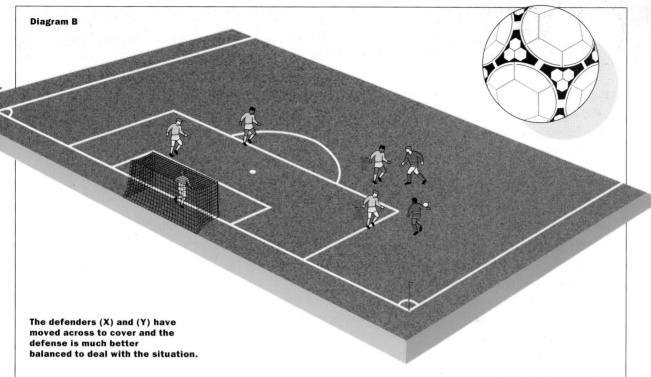

The defenders (X) and (Y) have
moved across to cover and the
defense is much better
balanced to deal with the situation.

Tight marking

When the opposition is in possession
your action should always be determined by the position of the ball. You
should either mark your opponent
closely, drop off to cover a teammate,
or pull away from your opponent to
keep your team's shape and balance.
The closer you are to the ball the
more closely you should mark.

Close support

Except when you have a
specific man-marking
role (when you follow
your opponent everywhere),
you should drop off from your opponent to cover a teammate who is
now moving in to mark tightly. Take
up a position close enough to support your teammate, ready to move
in and challenge if he is beaten.

You should also move up and mark
your designated attacker if the ball
is passed to him.

Defensive balance

If the ball is at a distance and
there is little opportunity for an
opponent to make a long pass to
the player you are marking, remain
alert and be prepared to support
your central defenders or provide
cover for a fullback. But be aware
of the man you are supposed to be
marking. He may be waiting for you
to move!

In Diagram A the defenders have
pushed back toward their own
goal, leaving an attacker
unmarked and in a good position
to shoot. In Diagram B, however,
the defenders are more aware of
the situation, having covered a

possible run, and are in better balance to deal with the attack.

Safety first

If you are challenged close to your
own goal, you shouldn't attempt to
skillfully dribble the ball into safety
or pass while under pressure, you
should clear your lines as quickly as
possible. The best way to do this is
to play it out of bounds.

The general rule here is "play the
way you are facing." It may seem a
negative tactic to kick the ball out of
bounds, or even give away a corner
kick, but it is better than to lose the
ball in the tackle (or by having your
pass intercepted) in the danger
zone. Many goals have been given
away by defenders trying to be too
clever in their own penalty area and
losing possession.

Man-for-man marking

There are two principal methods of defending: man-for-man and the zonal marking system. The man-for-man system (see Diagram A) is the most commonly used system among teams in the world.

Basically it involves one defender marking one attacker instead of patrolling a space or "zone." When the opposition is attacking, defenders must know which players they are responsible for and follow them closely. When an attack starts, the defense should quickly take up position, marking man-for-man, especially those opposing players close to the ball.

This is a slightly risky strategy without a spare player, because as soon as an attacker gets past his marker, the defense is outnumbered. If an attacker gets into the danger areas, as the nearest defender you should go for the tackle leaving other defenders to cover the player you would normally be marking. Insuring adequate defensive cover of the other attackers while the player in possession is being tackled is very important.

In Diagram B, when attacker (A) is being tackled by defender (X), defenders (Y) and (Z) are covering attackers (B) and (C).

(Y) and (Z) are positioned slightly behind (B) and (C) so they can react to any movement.

As (C) moves to (C1), (Z) also moves to (Z1) and is ready to intercept the ball or tackle (C).

If (A) dribbles past (X), the situation changes.

Three attackers (A), (B) and (C) are faced with only two defenders (Y) and (Z). If neither (Y) or (Z) leave their men to tackle (A), he will have a clear run to goal. But if (Y) leaves (B), then (A) can pass to (B) with little risk of interception.

The Zonal System

Zonal marking is an effective alternative to man-for-man marking and is often used by British League clubs.

In Diagram C defenders are responsible for guarding their area or zone of the pitch and marking any attacker who comes into it. Unlike man-for-man marking, where a defender will follow his opponent anywhere, the zonal system allows a defender to hand over responsibility to a teammate if an attacker crosses into the next zone.

Zonal marking requires good understanding between defenders, who must not be pulled out of position. They'll leave gaps if they stray too far out of their zone.

For example, a right winger running down the flank with the ball is marked by the leftback. If the winger moves inside and across the pitch he gets picked up by the defender in the next zone. A midfielder will, of course, need to cover the opposing winger.

Flat back four

This means having four defenders in a straight line across the back. Each player should hold position and pick up any attacker who comes into his zone. Because defenders are in a flat line they must be aware of runs from strikers and midfield players into forward areas.

If an attack comes down the right, the back four should move across in a line in that direction. The defend-

Diagram A

The man-for-man marking system provides solid defensive coverage, but is vulnerable if the ball is played into space.

Diagram B

While attacker (A) is
being tackled by
defender (X), defenders (Y) and (Z)
are covering attackers (B) and (C). If (A)
dribbles past (X), the situation changes.
Either (Y) or (Z) must leave their man to
tackle him or he will have a clear run at goal.

ers should be covering each other
and remain aware of the lack of pro-
tection on the field's left side.

If an attack comes through the
middle, the back four should move
into a pyramid formation, which
forces the attackers to play the ball
out wide. Good communication
between the back four players is
essential for the system to work
well. When it is safe to move up, or
to catch the opposition offside, the
central defender or goalkeeper
should give the order.

Those sides adopting a flat back
four frequently protect them with at
least one defensive central midfield
player. If possession of the ball is
lost during attack, the job of this
player is to make sure the back four
are not exposed to dangerous
attacks.

Funnel defense

When a team is pressed toward its
own goal, defenders should "funnel" opponents into crowded areas
in the center of the field. Fullbacks

stand on the sideline side of their
opponents, forcing them to go
inside where they have a better
chance to intercept the ball and
cover each other.

Funnel defense's advantages are:
that it stops opponents getting crosses in; means central defenders are
not pulled out of position; and attackers are caught offside. If the ball is
played behind the back four, the goalkeeper can come out and take it. This
system only works when midfielders
join central defenders at the back.

Diagram C

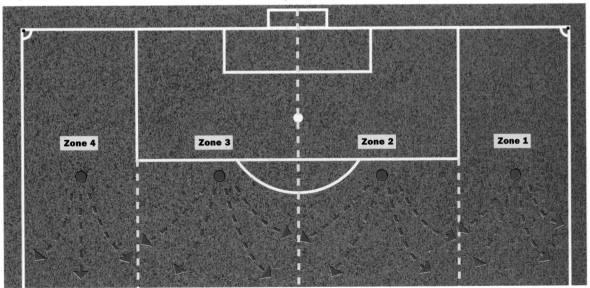

Zone 4　Zone 3　Zone 2　Zone 1

Man-for-man marking with a sweeper

A variation on the man-for-man marking system, the defense lines up with players marking their respective opponents. A lone player—called the sweeper—is placed behind the line, with the task of correcting any mistakes that might occur. He doesn't mark an attacker but acts as a safety valve to relieve attacking pressure by barring any opponent beating the defense line (see Diagram A).

As soon as the sweeper has the ball the players in the defense line will need to get free of the opponents they've previously been marking. Playing behind the defense, the sweeper has an overall view of the game and is in the best place to intercept through-balls, start counter-attacks with a long pass and even move forward as an extra attacker. From this rearguard position, the sweeper is also best placed to signal for the offside trap to be sprung.

The offside trap

Before the ball is played, the defense moves out in a line at a given signal (see Diagram B). This often catches attackers offside, or forces them to play the ball back toward their own half of the field.

Played correctly, the offside trap can prove an effective method of breaking up attacks and keeping the action as far away from the goal as possible.

Playing the offside trap requires good teamwork, communication and discipline. But teams should not use this tactic too often in a game. It frustrates the opposition and encourages attackers to take on opponents by dribbling straight through, or to beat the trap with quick passing movements. If an attacker breaks through the offside trap successfully with a carefully timed run, there is

often a clear path through to goal. In fact, many goals are scored by attackers beating the offside trap.

Defensive play at set-pieces

Free kicks can be dangerous attacking weapons because they present the opposition with the opportunity of bringing extra players forward to execute carefully planned moves. But they can be defended against.

Defenses are often caught out with a variety of pre-planned moves that result in goals. Set-piece situations are a real test of defenses and their organizational abilities.

There are a number of basic rules to follow when defending free kicks. They are:

(1) In training decide on which players your team will use to form a defensive wall in matches;

Diagram A

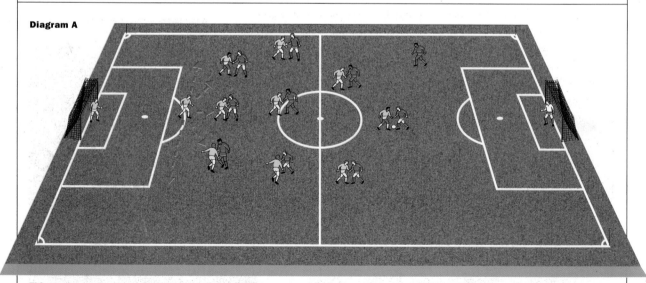

This system relies on man-for-man marking, with a sweeper playing a roving role behind his defense as a safety valve.

Diagram C

**Defenders move up in a
line at a given signal as
the ball is played.**

(2) Concentrate on the situation because many players lose concentration when the ball goes dead;

(3) Get as many players as possible back behind the ball and switch to man-for-man marking, otherwise the defending team could find itself outnumbered;

(4) Don't get distracted by the opposition moving around and calling to teammates;

(5) Be aware of threatening blind-side runs;

(6) Leave one player free to pounce on rebounds or clearances from the defensive wall.

Defending set-pieces

Building a wall

The "defensive wall" is built to protect the part of the goal which the goalkeeper might not be able to reach, as well as attackers' passing movements.

Defensive walls are needed when a direct, or indirect free kick has been awarded in a position from which a shot can prove dangerous. Although the goalkeeper usually organizes the wall (to provide a good cover from shots while retaining as clear a view as possible of the attackers) the keeper should not have sole responsibility. Another defender standing ten yards behind the kicker should judge the flight of the ball and direct the wall with the aid of the goalkeeper.

It's better if your defenders con-

**Wimbledon's five-man wall prepares
to face a free kick.**

centrate on marking opposing attackers—or picking up central defenders who have moved forward—rather than standing in the wall. Midfielders are the best players to have in a wall, with the tallest standing on the outside of the wall to block a swerving shot. The anchor player in second place should also be tall enough to counter the chip shot. This player must also insure that the wall is not pulled out of position.

The number of players in the wall should be decided by the goalkeeper. As a rule five are used to defend a kick that has been awarded in a central position near the penalty area (two should be enough for a kick taken from an acute angle at the side of the area). If the kick is indirect inside the penalty area six to seven players should form in the wall.

• The wall should be positioned to cover one side of the goal, allowing the goalkeeper a clear view of the ball from the other side.

• Despite what you may have seen, players in the wall should not link arms because this restricts their movement. However, there are two vital parts which should be protected (see picture below).

• If you're in the wall you should be brave and not duck, or twist your body when the kick is taken, no matter how hard the ball has been struck.

• While staying on the right side of the laws, prevent opponents from getting into your wall. An attacker can stand less than ten yards from the kick and move away from the wall at the critical moment, leaving a gap for the taker of the free kick to shoot through.

• If, when the kick is taken, the ball is pushed sideways, players in the wall should not be tempted to charge out of position as a unit. The wall should remain firm, while the defender at the end of the wall nearest the ball attacks it.

• If you manage to block the free kick, you should push out as quickly as possible. This is the ideal moment to take the initiative and launch a counter-attack, while the attacking team still has the majority of its players committed to your half. Your fullbacks should break quickly from defense, with the midfielders in support to either run with the ball or pass it accurately.

• When defending set-pieces, move quickly upfield once the kick has been cleared to deny attackers space and to catch them offside.

• Defending against free kicks taken from wide positions is much easier because a direct shot on goal is less likely. If the ball is positioned on either wing a cross will probably follow. In this situation a two-man wall should be enough to prevent a clear shot at goal.

Germany's Thomas Hässler (8) has the Belgian wall on red alert in their 1994 World Cup second round game.

Diagram A

This diagram shows the correct positioning for defending a near-post corner.

Defending at corners

The goalkeeper is the key player when defending corner kicks because he can catch the cross. He should stand just inside the far post a yard off his line and shout to tell his defenders if he is going to attack the ball. In crowded penalty areas, or for inswinging corners, the goalkeeper may prefer standing halfway across his goal.

Marking should be man-for-man, or zone with defenders positioned between their opponents and the ball but slightly in front of it to give them the space to attack the ball. A defender should be placed just inside each post, standing about a yard inside the post. From this position they can cover shots aimed at the corner of the goal and allow their goalkeeper room to attack the ball without blocking the view.

But some goalkeepers, Bruce Grobbelaar for example, like the six-yard box clear of defenders so that they have room to go for the ball.

For balls played toward the far post at corners, defenders should stand just outside the six-yard box, one in line with the far post and the other in line with the edge of the box and others marking either attackers or zones.

Defending at throw-ins

At short throw-ins the player receiving the ball will probably try to play the ball back to the thrower, so close down the receiver and mark the thrower to compromise this option.

Long throw-ins should be treated like corners and defended as such. Mark the space behind and in front of opponents likely to receive the ball and cut down space in the penalty area.

Defenders have two distinct advantages at long throw-ins: more time is taken by the thrower and it is generally clear where the ball will be delivered. Defenders are also given an opportunity to head the ball clear, since it's usually lofted high into the air toward their goal.

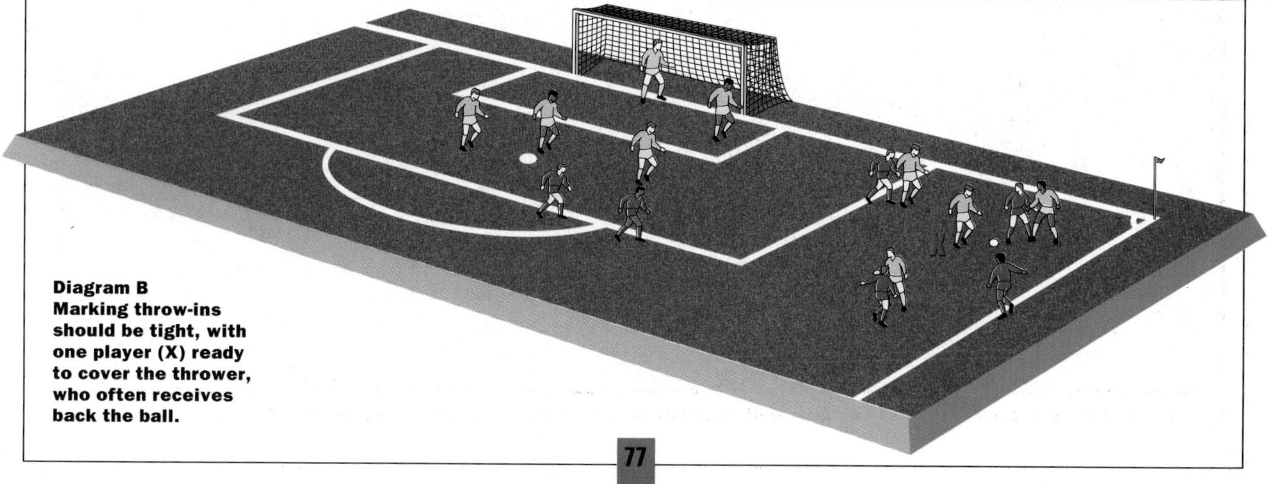

Diagram B
Marking throw-ins should be tight, with one player (X) ready to cover the thrower, who often receives back the ball.

Glossary

Advantage: When a referee decides not to award a free kick to a team because a stoppage would mean they would lose the advantage gained.

Anchor-man (Anchor-player): A mid-field player whose main role is to win the ball.

Angle: Applied to the direction in which the ball is traveling. Goalkeepers come off their line to "narrow the angle." Attackers will drop off opponents to make a better angle for a teammate. Defenders cut down the potential scoring area by moving to cover space between the attacker and the goal.

Back four: The four back defenders who form a line of defense in front of goal.

Back-heel: Striking or passing the ball with the back (heel) of the boot.

Ball watching: Watching the ball, or going for it, and not being aware where your opponent is running to or standing.

Bicycle kick: An acrobatic overhead kick (usually a volley) made with one's back to the target.

Blind side: The opposite side of a player to the ball, or an area outside your marker's line of vision.

Block tackle: A tackle made in an upright position, with the side of the foot facing the opponent.

Booking: See Caution

Box: The penalty area.

Caution: When the referee notes a player's name (and number, if any) for a number of offenses, either persistent misconduct or ungentlemanly conduct. After administering a caution (or booking as it is commonly known) the referee will show a yellow card.

Center-back: One or two defenders who guard the center of defense.

Channels: Areas of play on the pitch into which balls are played.

Chip: A pass made by a stabbing action of the kicking foot under the ball so that it gains height and not distance.

Close down: To deny an opponent space.

Committing a defender: Insuring that an opposing defender is brought into play by moving toward him.

Corner kick: A kick awarded to the attacking team when the ball goes out of play over the goal line and was last touched by an opponent.

Covering: When the opposition is in possession, taking a position behind your teammate, or marking a man or zone, in case he is beaten.

Cross: To play the ball from a wide position into a more central position.

Cross over: When two attacking players switch positions, having run past each other to confuse the opposition.

Cushion control: When a player stops the ball so that his body acts as a cushion to take the pace off the ball and allows it to drop to his feet. This can be done with the chest, the inside of the foot, or thigh.

The D: The arc marked outside the penalty area.

Dangerous play: When players raise either feet above waist height in a way that could cause injury to an opponent's head or upper body. The referee will award an indirect free kick for this infringement.

Dead-ball: When the ball is out of play, having crossed either goal line, the sidelines or when play is stopped by the referee for a foul.

Decoy run: When an attacker makes a run to take a defender out of position with the aim of creating space for a teammate.

Defender: A player whose main role is to prevent the opposition from scoring.

Deflecting: Changing the direction of the ball without stopping it.

Diagonal run: When players run at an angle either from the wing toward goal or from the middle toward the corner.

Dribbling: A player using ball control to take the ball past several opponents.

Dropped ball: When the referee, having stopped the game while the ball was still in play, restarts the game by dropping the ball between two opposing players. Players can touch the ball as soon as it touches the ground.

Dummy: When a player feints to move in one direction and then moves away in another.

Ejection: See Sending off

Extra time: A spell of extra play, usually 15 minutes each way, to decide a knockout game when the scores are level at the end of the normal 90 minutes play.

Far post: The goalpost furthest from where the ball is crossed.

Flank: See Wings

Flight: The trajectory of the ball.

Forward: An attacking player mainly concerned with creating and scoring goals. Also known as a striker.

Free kick (Direct): A free kick from which a goal can be scored without another player having touched the ball.

Free kick (Indirect): A free kick from which the ball must be touched by another player before a goal can be scored.

Fullback: A defender operating on either the right or left side of defense.

Goal side: A defensive position where you go so that you are between an attacker and your goal.

Goal area (or six-yard box): The 6yd x 20yd area directly in front of the goal from where goal kicks are taken.

Goal kick: A kick awarded to the defending team when the ball goes over the goal line (but not in the goal) and was last touched by an opponent.

Half-volley: When the ball is kicked just after it has made contact with the ground.

Hold: Retain possession of the ball.

Hustle: To put opponents under pressure when they have the ball.

Instep: The upper surface of the foot or boot by the big toe.

Injury time: Time added on by the referee to the end of each half to compensate for time lost when players were receiving treatment on the field, or when play stops. Injury time is decided by the referee.

Jockeying: When a defender retreats between an attacker and the goal forcing him to go in one particular direction while other defenders move in to cover.

Libero: The European name for a Sweeper (see Sweeper).

Man-for-man marking: When players exclusively mark one opponent.

Midfield player: A player who is neither an attacker nor a defender but links with and helps out both.

Narrowing the angle: When a goal-keeper advances toward an attacking player to cut down the amount of goal the attacker has to shoot at.

Near-post: The post nearest to where the ball is crossed.

Offside: When an attacker has less than two defenders in front of him and the ball is passed forward to him.

One touch: Passing the ball first time to a teammate without controlling it first.

One-two: See Wall pass

Overlap: When a player runs ahead and outside of a teammate in possession to offer space for a pass.

Own goal: When a goal is scored after last being touched by a member of the defending team.

Penalty area (18-yard box): The area in which a goalkeeper can handle the ball. If a defender commits an offense in this area that is punishable by a direct free kick a penalty kick is awarded.

Penalty kick: A direct kick at goal taken 12 yards from the goal's center. While it's being taken, all players except the goalkeeper and penalty taker must be outside the penalty area and the D.

Push pass: A pass made with the inside of the foot.

Run with the ball: When a player runs with the ball.

Running off the ball: When a player makes a run to support a teammate who has the ball.

Sending off: Players sent from the Field Of Play by the referee after committing serious foul play, violent conduct, using foul or abusive language, or persistent misconduct after a caution in the same game. To signal that a player is being sent off the referee shows the red card.

Set play: Any pre-planned move to restart play from a free kick, corner kick or throw-in.

Shielding the ball: Placing your body in such a way as to prevent an opponent seeing or playing the ball. This is not the same as Obstruction, however.

Sideline: The longer boundary line of the Field Of Play. When the ball crosses the sideline play is restarted by means of a throw-in.

Striker: An attacking player whose main role is to score goals.

Supporting player: A player who positions himself to receive a pass from a teammate in possession.

Sweeper: A defender who plays behind the other defenders, covering them and tidying up any defensive errors. He's also ideally positioned to launch counter-attacks.

Tackle: When a player makes a challenge and dispossess an opposing player or wins the ball himself with legal use of the feet.

Through-ball: A pass through the opposing defense for a teammate to chase.

Throw-in: Restarting play after the ball has gone over the sideline. The throw has to be taken by a member of the team that did not touch the ball last.

Turning the opponent: Forcing an opponent to turn by playing the ball past him.

Two touch: Passing the ball to a teammate after controlling it first.

Vision: A player's ability to see where other players are positioned and to understand the full range of passing options available.

Volley: Striking the ball while it's still in the air.

Wall: A barrier formed by players to block a free kick near their goal.

Wall pass: Also known as the "one-two." A quick pass is made to a teammate who immediately returns the ball to you. This is similar to kicking a ball at a wall and then playing the rebound.

Winger: A player who plays on the far left or right of the attack.

Wings: The areas of the pitch near the sideline.

Index

ITALICS INDICATES PICTURE